MOVING FORWARD
The provision of accommodation for Travellers and Gypsies

Heaven Crawley

30-32 Southampton Street, London WC2E 7RA
Tel: 020 7470 6100 Fax: 020 7470 6111
info@ippr.org
www.ippr.org
Registered charity 800065

The Institute for Public Policy Research (ippr), established in 1988, is Britain's leading independent progressive think tank. The values that drive our work include delivering social justice, deepening democracy, increasing environmental sustainability and enhancing human rights. Through our well-researched and clearly argued policy analysis, our publications, our media events, our strong networks in government, academia and the corporate and voluntary sector, we play a vital role in maintaining the momentum of progressive thought.

ippr's aim is to bridge the political divide between the social democratic and liberal traditions, the intellectual divide between the academics and the policy makers and the cultural divide between the policy-making establishment and the citizen. As an independent institute, we have the freedom to determine our research agenda. ippr has charitable status and is funded by a mixture of corporate, charitable, trade union and individual donations.

Research is ongoing, and new projects being developed, in a wide range of policy areas including sustainability, health and social care, social policy, citizenship and governance, education, economics, democracy and community, media and digital society and public private partnerships.

For further information you can contact ippr's external affairs department on info@ippr.org, you can view our website at www.ippr.org and you can buy our books from Central Books on 0845 458 9910 or email ippr@centralbooks.com.

Trustees

Chris Powell
(Chairman)

Professor Kumar
  Bhattacharyya
Lord Brooke
Lord Eatwell
Lord Gavron
Chris Gibson Smith
Professor Anthony
  Giddens
Lord Hollick

Chai Patel
(Secretary)

Jane Humphries
Roger Jowell
Neil Kinnock
Richard Lambert
Professor David
  Marquand
Frances O'Grady
David Pitt-Watson
Dave Prentis

Jeremy Hardie
(Treasurer)

Lord Puttnam
Sir Martin Rees
Jan Royall
Ed Sweeney
Baroness Williams
Baroness Young of
  Old Scone

Production & design by **EMPHASIS**
ISBN 1 86030 231 9
© IPPR 2004

Contents

About the author
Acknowledgements
Acronyms
Preface

	Summary of key recommendations	i
1.	Background and context	1
2.	Measuring and monitoring need	6
3.	Race and (in)equality issues	10
4.	Past and present policy for delivering accommodation	14
5.	Why we need to move forward	30
6.	A fresh approach to the provision of accommodation	39
7.	Conclusions and recommendations	54
	Endpiece	60
	Endnotes	62
	References	67
	Appendix 1: Round table seminar participants	69
	Appendix 2: Responses to the consultation paper	71
	Appendix 3: Labour Party conference fringe event participants	72

About the author

Dr Heaven Crawley is an Associate Director at the Institute for Public Policy Research where she runs the Migration and Equalities Programme. Before joining the ippr, Heaven was responsible for asylum and migration research at the Home Office Research and Statistics Directorate, and has worked extensively with the voluntary sector undertaking research on asylum policy and practice, particularly in relation to the experiences of women.

Acknowledgements

We would like to thank all of those who participated in the ippr seminars which were held as part of this research and enabled us to understand better the relationship between the different stakeholders with an interest in this issue. We would also like to thank all those who gave of their time and shared information with the researchers outside of these events, and in particular those Travellers and Gypsies who invited us to visit their homes, who responded to the consultation exercise and who contributed in other ways to our thinking and analysis.

There are a number of individuals who deserve particular recognition for their contribution to this report. We would particularly like to acknowledge the assistance of Jane Foot who undertook much of the initial research, and Andrew Ryder of the Traveller Law Reform Coalition who has provided support for much of the work that has been undertaken over the past year. In addition, particular thanks are due to Anne Bagehot (Gypsy Council), Sasha Barton (CRE), Rodney Bickerstaffe (Labour Party Campaign for Travellers' Rights), Sarah Cemlyn (University of Bristol), Cliff Codona (National Travellers Action Group), Janie Codona (National Travellers Action Group), Bill Forrester (Kent County Council, currently on secondment to the ODPM), Brian Foster (Inner London Traveller Education Consortium), Maureen Fraser (CRE), Trevor Phillips (CRE), Erik Shopland (Crawley Borough Council), Charles Smith (Gypsy Council and Labour Party Campaign for Travellers' Rights), Len Smith (Traveller Law Reform Coalition), Sarah Spencer (CRE), Seamus Taylor (CRE) and Patrice Van Cleemput (University of Sheffield).

ippr is grateful to the London Borough of Newham for the financial support they have provided towards this work, particularly in its early stages. We are particularly grateful to Councillor Richard Crawford, Bryn Griffiths, Malcolm Smith and John Lowe from the Overview and Scrutiny Unit for their contribution to the seminars and active engagement throughout the research process.

Despite the emerging consensus, there continues to be a wide range of views on how to address the issues that are the focus of this work and we have attempted to reflect these in the report. Final responsibility for the report's content and conclusions rests, of course, with the author.

Acronyms

ACERT	Advisory Council for the Education of Romany and other Travellers
CJPOA	Criminal Justice and Public Order Act (1994)
CRE	Commission for Racial Equality
DEFRA	Department for Environment, Food and Rural Affairs
DETR	Department of the Environment, Transport and the Regions
DfES (DfEE)	Department for Employment and Skills
LCTR	Labour Party Campaign for Travellers' Rights
LGA	Local Government Association
LGTU	London Gypsy and Traveller Unit
NDPB	Non-Departmental Public Body
Ofsted	Office for Standards in Education
ODPM	Office of the Deputy Prime Minister
RDA	Regional Development Agency
RRA	Race Relations (Amendment) Act (2000)
RSL	Registered Social Landlord
TLRC	Traveller Law Reform Coalition
TLRU	Traveller Law Research Unit, University of Cardiff

Preface

The lack of adequate site provision for Traveller and Gypsy communities and the associated problems arising from unauthorised encampments have emerged as issues of increasing and sometimes considerable concern for local authorities, neighbouring residents and Travellers and Gypsies in both rural and urban areas. Policy debate has focused primarily on the tension between the duty of local authorities' adequately to meet the needs of Traveller and Gypsy communities and their responsibility to respond to the concerns of local residents and promote the economic, environmental and social well being of their communities. These tensions have been particularly evident over recent months with the tragic death of a young Traveller, Johnny Delaney, in Cheshire and the scenes at Firle in East Sussex where an effigy of a Traveller family was burnt at a public bonfire night.

Ironically these events have taken place at a time when there is more interest than ever in resolving, once and for all, the problems of inadequate accommodation provision for Traveller and Gypsy families. The work of the Traveller Law Reform Coalition combined with recent and on-going reviews of existing policy and practice within ODPM and a revitalised and more explicit commitment by the CRE to addressing the discrimination and inequalities experienced by Travellers and Gypsies has, for the first time, provided hope that long-term answers will be found and that racism and local tensions between the Travelling and settled communities can be reduced.

We hope that the research undertaken by ippr will contribute to this progress. During the course of the research, we created a political space within which seemingly intractable problems could be addressed by a range of stakeholders and policy makers. Our aim has been to help build consensus about the need to provide sufficient permanent and transit sites for Travellers and Gypsies. We believe that providing such accommodation is the key to tackling a wider range of social and environmental problems experienced by Traveller and Gypsy families and the communities in which they currently reside.

This report synthesises policy thinking over the past year. Whilst there remains some way to go in ensuring that the policy debate translates into real and lasting change on the ground, we hope that it will serve to bring closer the delivery of appropriate accommodation for Travellers and Gypsies.

Nick Pearce
Acting Director

Summary of key recommendations

This report sets out the issues relating to the provision of accommodation for Travellers and Gypsies including what has gone before, and the consequences of the existing approach for the Travelling community, for local authorities, and for those parts of the settled community affected by unauthorised encampments. It sets out a framework for addressing current and projected need based on the provision of public sites through mainstreamed housing provision and improved planning procedures to facilitate the appropriate development of private sites by Travellers and Gypsies. It suggests that the solutions to addressing the current inadequacies of accommodation (both quantity and quality) lie in: ensuring that the existing obligations to ensure equality of access to public provision and promote good race relations are properly utilised as a lever for change; in reforms of government planning and housing strategies which can provide a vehicle to ensure that Traveller and Gypsy accommodation needs are properly resourced and enforced; and in the on-going ODPM review of its own Travellers and Gypsies Strategy.

It is clear from the research undertaken for this report that any lasting and forward looking policy solution will need to be one that:

- Recognises the entitlement of Travellers and Gypsies like other residents to accommodation which, in their case, includes sufficient sites, both permanent and transit;

- Provides a funding mechanism where specific funds are channelled into providing suitable accommodation for Travellers and Gypsies, similar to other forms of social housing;

- Establishes a mechanism for enforcement which provides rewards as well as sanctions to local authorities;

- Recognises the challenges for local authorities but overcomes any inertia or resistance;

- Enables joined up regional accommodation provision;

- Allows flexibility of accommodation types to meet a range of needs;

- Is underpinned by a thorough needs assessment, building in projected needs;

- Facilitates the widespread identification and dissemination of good practice; and
- Is supported from initial outline to implementation by active involvement and meaningful consultation with Travellers and Gypsies.

We do not underestimate the scale of the challenge involved in addressing the issue of providing accommodation for Travellers and Gypsies but our research indicates that there are new opportunities ahead to make real and sustainable progress on the key issue of accommodation provision. Our specific recommendations are as follows:

- Permanent residential and transit sites should be classed as housing, for provision to be made through Regional Housing Strategies and Regional Spatial Strategies, and for funding to be provided through Regional Housing Boards; and for Regional Development Agencies to co-ordinate and lead local authorities in establishing networks of sites across each region, dependent on evidenced need.
- Local authorities thus would be required to make provision for sites within their Local Development Frameworks; for Regional Housing Boards to make receipt of funding for social housing dependent on an authority's willingness to provide the full package of housing required, including locations for suitable Travellers' sites.
- The sites should be established and run by local authorities, RSLs, private or voluntary bodies.
- A specialised national or regional RSL should be established for that purpose.
- This agenda should be driven forward by a high-level unit within the ODPM, led by a senior civil servant, charged with delivery of the necessary number of sites within Local Development Frameworks by 2006/7, and with the related responsibilities for promoting good practice and advice that we have proposed.
- This unit should be advised by a Traveller Task Force comprising

a significant proportion of Traveller and Gypsy representatives and other key stakeholders, who would be consulted at an early stage and ongoing, in a meaningful way, on any developments and advise the proposed unit.

- Local authorities should include Romany Gypsies and Irish Travellers in the Equalities Standard as a matter of urgency and ensure that all other local strategies include a recognition of – and response to – the needs of Travelling communities. It would be advisable for both local authorities still needing to produce Homelessness Strategies and those that already have produced these strategies to review them, to ensure full compliance with the requirements of the Race Relations (Amendment) Act (2000).

1. Background and context

Lack of suitable and adequate accommodation is consistently and increasingly identified as the most significant issue for many Travellers and Gypsies in England and Wales today. Our work indicates that Travelling and settled communities often have very different interests and that local authorities have dealt with the tensions that arise between the two with limited success. Traveller communities themselves fear that as long as there is no duty for local authorities to provide or facilitate secure sites, then the refurbishment grant that has been provided by the Government for the maintenance of existing sites will make no significant difference. Local authorities, meanwhile, remain convinced that without an increase in their powers to deal with the environmental damage and anti-social behaviour associated with some unauthorised encampments and some unauthorised developments (where planning permission has not been granted), they will be unable to persuade the settled community of the need to provide permanent residential and transit sites in their area.

What has emerged from this research, however, is a consensus among all of those involved in these issues that the time for permanent and sustainable solutions to the problems raised in this report is long over due. Not only is there increasing recognition of the need to make progress but there is also a developing consensus on how it might be achieved. Travellers and Gypsies themselves have created much of this momentum for change. Although there is clearly the potential for frustration and concern that 'we have been here before',[1] the emergence of the Traveller Law Reform Coalition marks a significant development in that it brings together many diverse groups around a common key priority, namely that of securing the implementation of the Traveller Law Reform Bill. Whilst the Bill (introduced in July 2002) was itself a Private Members Bill, and therefore could not be guaranteed a passage through Parliament, its major clauses in relation to accommodation have influenced the developing policy debate, particularly on the need to resolve accommodation issues as the key to progress on wider fronts.

At the same time there are new challenges and opportunities offered by policy and law at both central and local government levels, in the form of the 2004 Housing Bill, changes to planning legislation, the Anti-Social Behaviour Act (2003) and the Office of the Deputy Prime

Minister's (ODPM) own policy review to assess the impact of present policy and make recommendations for future policy. All of this is taking place in the context of the recently strengthened Race Relations (Amendment) Act (2000) – which imposes a public duty on local authorities and other public bodies to actively promote good race relations and provides a lever to promote change across the public sector – and government consultation over the amalgamation of the EU Framework Directive on Anti-Discrimination measures. Most recently, there has been a new and explicit commitment by the Commission for Racial Equality (CRE) to address the underlying causes of discrimination and hostility experienced by Travellers and Gypsies who fall within their remit. The CRE launched a consultation on its strategy for Travellers and Gypsies in October 2003 (to be published imminently), and is producing a work plan that will set out its work on this issue over the next three years. Speaking about the launch, Trevor Phillips, CRE Chair said:

> The launch of this consultation is a major step forward for the CRE in trying to find out more about and act upon the appalling levels of discrimination faced by Gypsies and Travellers. For this group, Great Britain is still like the American Deep South for black people in the 1950s. Extreme levels of public hostility exist in relation to Gypsies and Travellers – fuelled in part by irresponsible media reporting of the kind that would be met with outrage if it was targeted at any other ethnic group.[2]

The CRE's strategy demonstrates a commitment not just to identifying the discrimination faced by Travellers and Gypsies, but also taking concerted action to promote change. It is a vehicle for ensuring that its work on this issue is targeted, strategic and effective, identifying specific priority areas and selecting the particular actions that will have most impact.

Despite the many hurdles to overcome, it is clear that the time is ripe for pushing this agenda forward and to exploit the opportunity, for everyone, that exists to effect concrete and lasting change. This report does not specifically deal with the detailed issues of site provision. (These include who should be managing sites, where such sites should be located, how local authorities can work more closely with Travellers and Gypsies, the management of relationships with the police and others and the issue of how to ensure that the planning system is fair and effective and not over-influenced by simple public hostility.) Rather it provides an overall framework for better public provision and planning practice which will enable policy makers and practitioners at the national and local government level to move forward policy development in this area.

This report is the result of research undertaken by ippr to identify policy solutions and levers for ensuring that Travellers and Gypsies in the UK are able to access appropriate accommodation to meet their needs, either through the public provision of sites or through the ability to purchase and develop their own sites in appropriate locations. The aims of the project were:

- To foster the 'policy space' for debating these issues at the appropriate local, regional and national levels;

- To contribute to the policy debate on the balance of rights and responsibilities of Travellers and Gypsies; and

- To recommend innovative and pragmatic policy options for managing the environmental impact of Travelling communities.

The project consisted of research with Travellers and Gypsies and those representing their interests which was undertaken with the assistance of Jane Foot, an independent research consultant, and two round table seminars, held under Chatham House rules, on 28 November 2002 and 14 February 2003. These seminars brought together practitioners, academics, government and local authority officials, and representatives of the Travelling community, to explore the scope of the problem and key concerns (Seminar 1), and discuss possible policy solutions (Seminar 2). Ongoing meetings and discussions have been held with key stakeholders working in this area and with representatives from the Traveller and Gypsy communities since that time. Details of all those who participated in the seminars are included at Appendix 1.

A working paper specifically looking at the environmental impacts of unauthorised encampments was produced for the London Borough of Newham in March 2003. However, we realised at that stage that the work had already started to contribute to the development of a broader policy discussion about how to ensure suitable accommodation, both permanent and temporary, for Travellers and Gypsies and so address the root causes of unauthorised encampments, tackle some of the broader issues of social welfare (including health and education), and improve relations between Travelling and non-travelling communities.

As a result, we issued a consultation paper in July 2003 setting out some of the options for meeting the accommodation needs of Travellers and Gypsies, responses to which helped shape the content of this report. We were particularly interested in receiving feedback from Travellers and Gypsies and the groups by whom they are represented. Those who are not Travellers or Gypsies have traditionally had by far the greater say in this debate taking up – sometimes reasonably and understandably – issues of encampments and opposition to site proposals with their elected representatives. Those representatives have then pursued the issues of concern with more senior representatives, including those in Parliament. Because of their nomadic lifestyles, and living arrangements apart from others, Travellers and Gypsies present particular challenges when engaging – or seeking to engage – in consultation, inclusion and engagement strategies. Yet in order to understand and respond appropriately to the needs of Travellers and Gypsies it is essential that meaningful consultation is undertaken with their representatives, and also, ideally, with them directly, when formulating policy solutions. A list of those who responded to the consultation paper is provided in Appendix 2.

The feedback from the consultation exercise, combined with on-going discussions across government about the issue of accommodation provision led us to believe that there was merit in bringing together a further discussion of relevant stakeholders and interest groups. Together with the Traveller Law Reform Coalition we facilitated a fringe event at the Labour Party conference in Bournemouth in October 2003 to take forward discussions about the workability of ippr's proposals for accommodation provision. A list of participants is provided in Appendix 3.

Much of our work on the accommodation for Travellers and Gypsies has coincided with the ODPM's consultation on Guidance to local authorities and police forces on policy and practice towards unauthorised encampments, including new powers in the Anti-Social Behaviour Act (2003) (due to be published shortly), and has drawn on the seminars and discussions that were undertaken as part of that consultation exercise. It also coincided with DEFRA's consultation on reconfiguring statutory powers and responsibilities associated with achieving cleaner public spaces and local environments. Most significantly, the work was undertaken in the context of – and derived considerable benefit from – the extensive work undertaken and produced by the Traveller Law Reform Coalition connected with the recent Private Members' Traveller Law Reform Bill, the new All-Party Group of MPs (Chaired by Kevin McNamara MP) on this issue and of the growing concerns of the Commission for Racial Equality (CRE).

Traveller and Gypsy communities continue to be over-represented in nearly all indices of deprivation and social exclusion and to experience widespread prejudice and discrimination. Significant change will be needed in order to make a real impact on the lives of the Travelling community. As with other socially excluded groups it is clear that suitable, good quality, well-managed and regulated accommodation is the key to overcoming other social problems. Accommodation is inextricably linked to, and impacts upon, race relations, health, educational and employment outcomes, and relations with local authorities and the police. This report suggests that the key to this change is firmly to embed debates and policy development in this area in the wider mainstream equalities and community cohesion agenda.

2. Measuring and monitoring need

Who are the Travellers?

Estimates of the size of Britain's Traveller and Gypsy population vary. The Council of Europe has estimated it to be 300,000 (with 200,000 in settled housing) (Leigeois 1987). More recently Morris and Clements (2002) estimated the size of the community at 'no more than 300,000'. This would mean that Travellers and Gypsies may be similar in size to Britain's Bangladeshi community (280,000), and substantially smaller than the Black Caribbean and Indian communities. At present the only means of data collection is the twice-yearly Gypsy count, co-ordinated by the Office of the Deputy Prime Minister in England and the Gypsy Traveller count co-ordinated by the Scottish Executive in Scotland.[3]

Travellers and Gypsies are generally considered to consist of three distinct groups (Kenrick and Clark 1999):[4]

- Romany Gypsies who are estimated to be around 63,000 in the UK and a recognised ethnic minority group;

- Irish Travellers (estimated to be 19,000 living in Britain) with strong connections to Ireland and travelling regularly between the UK and Irish Republic, also recognised as an ethnic minority; and

- New Travellers, on which there is no information about numbers, and who are not recognised as an ethnic minority.[5]

These three groups constitute very distinct communities with little or no mixing between them. In addition there is a population of European Roma refugees and asylum seekers in the UK, most of whom are currently living in temporary accommodation and not seeking places on sites. This group is not included in the analysis undertaken for this research as it clearly has distinct needs.

The main social unit of the Traveller and Gypsy communities is the extended family; most camps (both official and unauthorised) are organised around extended family groups with many households in the group. Although the principle of nomadism is important for all Travellers and Gypsies, it is not clear what proportion of movement is driven by the desire for nomadism (including the search for employment) and what proportion of travel takes place in response to the non-toleration policies of local authorities and forced removal at the request of local communities who do not want Travellers and Gypsies in their areas. Whilst only some sites generate crime or pollution (and only a very few in serious measure), this remains the main reasons given by local communities to their hostility to Travellers and can result in the majority of families being treated in the same way. Reflecting this, it is not clear what proportion of Travellers and Gypsies who have moved into 'bricks and mortar' permanent housing have done so because of the lack of alternatives available to them and would return to some form of nomadism if the provision of suitable accommodation made this a possibility.

It is not inconceivable that the failure to develop a national policy of accommodation provision for Travellers and Gypsies reflects an implicit assumption that those in Travelling communities will eventually choose to move into permanent 'bricks and mortar' housing and will no longer travel. This general assumption, which was partly behind the passing of the Caravan Sites Act (1968) and appeared again in the review of policy in 1992 which led to the Criminal Justice and Public Order Act (1994), is not supported by the available evidence, although many families do move into housing, sometimes willingly, sometimes not. Nonetheless, it continues to have many implications for policy in this area, not only regarding the provision of sites but also in terms of service provision and delivery, including health and education. The situation is further complicated by the fact that when asked about their accommodation preferences, many Travellers and Gypsies indicate that their preference would be a bungalow or mobile chalet (preferably on their own land). It appears that the aversion is not necessarily to bricks and mortar *per se* but to the design of social housing, which is not appropriate to the extended family and community lifestyle. It is also clear that some of those who wish to live in bungalows or mobile homes want the space to keep a mobile home or caravan which would enable them to travel at certain times of the year for social or employment purposes.

Data and monitoring gaps

Before embarking on an analysis of the issue of accommodation provision, it should be noted that there is a significant lack of data and information about Traveller and Gypsy communities. Since Travellers and Gypsies are not defined as a census category, there is little or no data on population sizes and geographical locations. Services that forecast needs and demand based on census data will similarly not account for Travellers and Gypsies. Although estimates exist from both empirical research and local authority caravan counts (collated by ODPM), there is insufficient evidence on the scale and nature of site provision required. It was suggested during the seminar discussions that those figures that do exist are insufficiently detailed. For example, to establish 'need' it would be helpful if count figures distinguished between planning consent disputes and other unauthorised encampments. This is particularly important and necessary for rural authorities where Travelling communities have purchased their own land. Meanwhile as indicated above, the extent to which Travellers and Gypsies are resident in permanent housing because of the lack of alternatives available to them is largely unknown, although it has been estimated by the Council of Europe and the Gypsy Council to be around 200,000 in the UK as a whole (Thomas and Campbell 1992, Morris and Clements 2002). Similarly, the extent of projected need arising, in part, from migration into the UK from the Republic of Ireland and accession states entering the EU in May 2004 in which there is a significant Roma Gypsy population remains largely unquantified. Across all of these data needs there exists a common problem of accuracy resulting from the fact that many Travellers and Gypsies have deep-rooted fears about identifying their ethnicity because of existing prejudice and discrimination.

The absence of official national figures on the size of the Traveller and Gypsy population is replicated by a lack of systematic ethnic data collection across key areas of service provision and employment. Because Travelling communities are often not included as a category in ethnic monitoring schemes of local authorities and statutory agencies, planning service delivery at local levels (such as housing, social services, health) does not take adequate account of their needs. The exception is school pupil data. A Thematic Regulation study commissioned by

Communities Scotland in 2002 into services for Travellers and Gypsies found that all councils showed weaknesses in a range of areas, including inadequate needs assessment and lack of long-term planning for site improvements, financial planning and setting and monitoring service standards.[6] The evidence base which does exist arises from a number of studies on discrete aspects of the Traveller and Gypsy experience such as accommodation; education, health and well-being; the work of Travellers' and Gypsies' voluntary organisations and the individual cases brought to bodies like the CRE. These specific studies consistently paint a picture of intense and stark inequality and disadvantage whether in relation to accommodation, health, education or public attitudes.

In addition it is clear from our limited work on this issue that there is insufficient monitoring about the outcomes for Travellers and Gypsies:

- No monitoring of engagement or consultation with public bodies so that information on needs can be collated and satisfaction with services can be responded to;

- No monitoring of service take up or outcomes, except in relation to education; and

- No monitoring of crime statistics to identify the extent to which Travellers and Gypsies are both victims and perpetrators of crime.

In the current climate of evidence-based resource allocation and reliance on performance data and targets to drive public service delivery, the lack of data means there are no levers to pull to gain priority for these services in competition with other pressing local needs. Traveller and Gypsy organisations have frequently raised the need for Travellers and Gypsies to be included as a distinct category in ethnic monitoring systems in order to help overcome the challenges raised in establishing their needs. Without this data it will be difficult for the Audit Commission to ascertain whether local authorities are fulfilling their requirements under the Race Relations (Amendment) Act (2000) to both provide services on a non-discriminatory basis and promote good relations and race equality.[7]

3. Race and (in)equality issues

The absence of appropriate data to measure and monitor the provision of accommodation and services for Travellers and Gypsies is in significant part a reflection of the failure to acknowledge and respond appropriately to the different lifestyles of the Travelling community. At even a more basic level, however, it reflects a widespread failure to recognise and respond to Travellers and Gypsies as an ethnic minority group covered by the existing legislative provisions for racial equality.

There is evidence that the needs of Travellers and Gypsies are currently not sufficiently integrated into 'mainstream' provision at both the central and local government levels including housing and homelessness strategies, planning regulations, social exclusion and community cohesion strategies, community safety strategies and local strategic partnerships. Housing law has rarely so far covered sites, and caravan sites, of all types, have quite different laws that apply to them. The security of tenure position is also quite different. Travellers and gypsies on public sites have less security than any other caravan site residents, and can legally be evicted from a site on which they have lived for many years with only 28 days or even less notice, and without, necessarily, any detailed examination of any allegations against them, as would happen with public housing tenants, providing that the evicting body has acted 'reasonably'. New policies – for example, the recent Disability Facilities Grant – regularly do not cover those living on such sites, although the Government has recently announced plans to remedy this particular anomaly soon.[8] At the same time, guidance on community cohesion published by the Home Office has very little to say on the experiences of the Travelling community and how to resolve and reduce local conflict.[9] As well as having discriminatory impacts on Travellers and Gypsies, it clearly makes the task of managing such sites, if there are problem individuals living there, that much harder for those employed to do so.

Perhaps the most obvious example of a failure to mainstream the needs of Travellers and Gypsies into existing policies can be seen in relation to homelessness. Under Section 1 of the Homelessness Act (2002) local authorities are required to carry out a homelessness review of their district and formulate and publish a Homelessness Strategy based on the results of that review.[10] Many authorities have already carried out homelessness reviews and produced their Homelessness Strategies as required under the Act.

However, Lord Avebury, a Liberal Democrat peer, (with assistance from representatives of the Children's Society) recently undertook a survey of 157 local authorities showing unauthorised encampments in the last bi-annual count of caravans. The survey looked at the authorities' Homelessness Strategies and whether Travellers were included within them. Eight authorities appear not to have produced strategies at all. Of the 137 authorities that did produce strategies, 72 per cent failed to make any reference to Travellers at all, despite having reported unauthorised encampments in the last bi-annual count. The research also found that there was no indication of any strategies for consultation with national or local Traveller organisations, or of advice being given by the authority's own Traveller or Gypsy officers (Avebury 2003).

The fact that hardly any of the authorities surveyed by Avebury made reference to their Race Equality Schemes in relation to Travellers and Gypsies reflects a bigger problem. Many local authorities (as well as much of the general public) are not aware that most Travelling communities are covered by the terms of the Race Relations (Amendment) Act (2000), which introduced a general duty on all public bodies to eliminate unlawful racial discrimination and to promote equality of opportunity and good race relations between people of different racial groups. Since 31 May 2003, an enforceable race equality duty has applied to 43,000 public bodies in England and Wales, and since November 2003 to approximately 350 public bodies in Scotland. The Act applies to all local authorities, schools, health bodies, criminal justice agencies and central government departments, all of which are key bodies impacting upon and interacting with Traveller and Gypsy communities. It applies to both Romany Gypsies and Irish Travellers who are recognised as distinct ethnic minorities.

The new duty has the potential to address some of the issues facing Travellers and Gypsies that are discussed in this report because it uniquely requires – and balances – a concern with tackling inequality and the promotion of good race relations. This balance is critical to making progress on this agenda given that relations between the Travelling and settled communities are sometimes fragile and may reflect deep-seated racism and prejudice against Travellers and Gypsies.

Hostile and racist attitudes towards Travellers and Gypsies are common amongst the general public. In a recent representative poll conducted by MORI, more than one third of respondents – which equates to about 14 million adults in England – admitted being prejudiced against Travellers and Gypsies. Respondents stated that they felt more prejudiced towards Travellers and Gypsies than they did towards lesbians and gay men, other ethnic minorities and disabled people (Stonewall 2003). Discriminatory signs and adverts in the 1960s in part prompted the initial race relations legislation. Yet overtly discriminatory 'No Travellers' or 'No Caravan-Dwellers' signs are still widespread.

Conflicts between the Travelling and settled communities over unauthorised encampments and other issues have exacerbated existing prejudices leading to an increasing number of racist (as defined by the police) incidents including the tragic death of the fifteen year old Traveller, Johnny Delaney.[11] Recent events at Firle in East Sussex which saw the burning of an effigy of a caravan complete with Traveller family and PIKEY number plate reflected tensions and frustrations which had arisen as a result of an unauthorised encampment on a local farmers' field. Irresponsible media reports can fuel hostile attitudes, and make it more difficult for public authorities charged with responding to the issues raised such as unauthorised encampments or site location.

There is clearly a complex interplay between the issue of inadequate accommodation, unauthorised encampments, deteriorating community relations and expressions of racist public attitudes. 'Nimbyism' (not in my back yard syndrome) is widespread, real and deep-seated and any strategy in this area cannot afford to ignore it. This racism and hostility cannot be condoned, but it shows that unless the accommodation issue is tackled, hostility will remain and good community relations cannot be fostered. Simply improving accommodation provision will not solve everything else, but it is certainly a necessary starting point. This is not to say that Travellers and Gypsies do not have any responsibility to ensure that they behave in appropriate ways. Each member of his or her community has the same responsibility as every other citizen. But the fact that a small minority from these communities behaves in ways that are then used to validate such intense discrimination against *all* Travellers and Gypsies is no more justifiable than it would be for any other ethnic minority group.

Our research on this issue, and specifically on unauthorised encampments, has concluded that responses to anti-social behaviour and the needs of the Traveller community need to be completely separated. Anti-social behaviour and criminality are commonly seen as symptomatic of deprivation and exclusion, irrespective of which section of the community a person comes from. There is an unacceptable and persistent culture of linking anti-social behaviour and the accommodation needs of Travellers and Gypsies. Accommodation needs and anti-social behaviour are two completely separate issues and they must be dealt with as such, irrespective of the pressure, both political and social, to link the two. As was pointed out by many of those with whom we consulted during the course of this research, this is not done with any other section of the community and would be considered racist under any other circumstances. Equally, however, the public bodies charged with enforcing against such anti-social and criminal behaviour as does exist should operate without fear or favour and treat Traveller and Gypsy communities and individuals with the same respect as they should treat everyone else. It is encouraging that a growing number of Travellers and Gypsies are now actively or tacitly supporting effective action against others who engage in any sort of crime or anti-social behaviour.

The challenge now is to mainstream effectively Traveller and Gypsy issues into the work of key public bodies on race equality so that it delivers real results. It is clear from the evidence that was collected during the course of this research that the potential of the race equality duty to tackle and reduce inequalities experienced by Travellers and Gypsies to ensure their inclusion in mainstream policy and provision is yet to be realised. Only by meeting the needs of Travellers and Gypsies in a way that minimises tension with the resident community will local authorities be complying with their duties under the existing legislation not only to ensure race equality in service delivery but also to promote good race relations.

4. Past and present policy for delivering accommodation

The provision of adequate and appropriate accommodation is of central concern to Traveller and Gypsy communities and often underlies their current poor quality of life and the local conflicts arising from unauthorised encampments. Some council sites are recorded as 'temporarily closed' or have fallen into terminal disrepair and are unusable, and many are in unsuitable or unsafe locations. Those Travellers and Gypsies who have no alternative but to live on unauthorised encampments, often lack basic facilities and experience difficulty in accessing adequate healthcare, education and other welfare services. They may also be subject to abuse and hostility from local residents.

The shortage of accommodation (in the form of sites) for Travellers and Gypsies has existed probably since early in the twentieth century, and perhaps before. Until the end of the Second World War, Travelling communities had a network of traditional stopping places often located near casual agricultural employment, especially fruit and hop picking; others made a living from scrap dealing and other forms of trading. The annual calendar of traditional cultural events and markets, together with employment opportunities determined travelling patterns. Camps were usually tolerated. There is, however, evidence that the combined effect of legislation and increasing pressure on land use has been to reduce considerably the availability of both stopping places and residential sites available to Travellers and Gypsies and their families. As pressures to find appropriate authorised sites have increased, the location of sites has become increasingly regulated through a series of legislative measures. Public sites provided before and (mainly) after the Caravan Sites Act (1968) have clearly reduced the shortfall, but solutions have always concentrated on meeting a finite need (which may in any case be underestimated because of the data gaps which were discussed earlier in this report), not recognising growing families, new household formation and the wish of many Travellers and Gypsies to live in caravans and mobile homes, despite the shortage of decent, legal and suitable sites and other obstacles. This reflects a distinct lack of realistic long-term planning and the absence of any clear, widely understood national policy towards accommodation for Travellers and Gypsies.

The scale of the need

In part because of the absence of appropriate data and monitoring outlined in Chapter 2, the detailed needs of Travellers and Gypsies for permanent housing and to cater for nomadism are largely unknown. The types of accommodation currently used include official or unauthorised transit sites, traditional stopping places, legally-established permanent residential sites (publicly owned and rented out, or owner occupied sites), and unauthorised encampments, which can range from Travellers and Gypsies who live on their own land but without planning permission, to tolerated sites, and unacceptable camps on public parks and car parks.

Available evidence produced for the ODPM by Pat Niner (2002) highlights a range of problems facing Travellers and Gypsies that are closely related to accommodation, including:

- Lack of authorised places to reside which leads to unauthorised encampments in unsuitable locations and associated environmental damage (whether perceived or real) that in turn can have a significant impact on community relations. There is evidence of families stopping on others' land, without consent. Because there are no facilities in place such encampments are often associated with domestic refuse and discarded waste, and sometimes with other kinds of waste, for example, abandoned cars and building rubble. There is also evidence of increasing unauthorised development (the development of land without prior planning permission).

- Inadequately serviced encampments with limited or non-existent portable toilets, domestic rubbish collection or water supply.

- Planning permission refusals. The vast majority of all initial planning applications are approved, but the vast majority of initial applications made by Travellers and Gypsies are refused, meaning that many Travellers and Gypsies cannot legally live on their own land because they have no planning permission.

- Poor location of publicly provided sites which are often found in polluted and hazardous environments on land which would not be developed for housing and which is entirely unsuitable for children. Recent research commissioned by ODPM (Niner 2002) indicates that existing public sites are often located at a distance from common services and near to motorways or major roads (26 per cent) railways (13 per cent), rubbish tips (12 per cent) and industrial or commercial activity (8 per cent) and sewage works (3 per cent).

- Lack of security of tenure and the threat of eviction on public sites. Travellers and Gypsies are not tenants but licensees on publicly provided sites and can be evicted from a site that they may have lived on for 20 years at one month's notice, providing the evicting public landlord acts 'reasonably'.

- Inadequate consultation and involvement of Travellers and Gypsies in site provision, location, design and management decisions.

The count carried out by local authorities in January 2002 showed a total of 13,612 Traveller or Gypsy caravans in England. Of these, 45 per cent were on authorised local authority owned sites and a further 34 per cent were on privately owned authorised sites. The remaining 2,774 caravans (20 per cent) were on unauthorised encampments on private land, the roadside, industrial estates and public open spaces.[12] Research undertaken for ODPM on the provision and condition of local authority sites indicates that between 1000 and 2000 additional residential pitches will be needed over the next five years and that between 2000 and 5000 additional pitches will be needed on transit sites to accommodate nomadism (Niner 2002). However, there is some concern within the Travelling community that the focus on transit sites will undermine recognition of the need for good quality permanent residential provision. According to the Gypsy Council, between 4000 and 5000 pitches are needed on permanent residential sites in next five years.

The Government's figures are also generally considered by Travellers and Gypsies to be an underestimate because they do not allow for the significant number who have been forced to move into permanent housing because of the lack of alternative provision. As was noted earlier in this report, some Travellers and Gypsies have adopted a completely settled lifestyle and live in 'bricks and mortar' social housing and private rented housing but it is not clear whether this is through choice or as a result of the shortage of sites (permanent and transit) on which to reside. It is anticipated that an unknown proportion of these would move back into a more nomadic way of life if the facilities were available. Despite the lack of agreement about the exact scale of the need, what is clear is that even if the number of pitches on permanent sites ran into the tens of thousands (which seems unlikely given all the available evidence) it would still pale into insignificance compared with the estimated 440,000 people who are currently homeless in the UK (including many families) and the vast amount of resource and political effort currently being devoted to building new homes to meet the needs of the settled community. It is also clear that the extent of the gap in current accommodation provision between the settled and Travelling communities is significant and probably growing. According to figures from the ODPM released in January 2003, nearly 22 per cent of the Traveller and Gypsy population who were, at that time, living in caravans or mobile homes were not on a legal site when counted compared with only 0.6 per cent of the settled population being homeless.

Perhaps one of the strongest points to emerge from the research was the need to recognise that, like all populations, Traveller and Gypsy needs vary hugely within communities and change with economic circumstances and over individual and family life cycles. These needs should be reflected in the range of accommodation being provided. Many Travellers and Gypsies want a permanent place to stay between periods of travel. Most Travellers and Gypsies want to be settled in winter, and there are examples of families living in unsatisfactory conditions in order to avoid moving before the spring. It was emphasised that unappealing transit sites should not be seen as the solution. The quality and suitability of accommodation that is fit for purpose, and its quality of self-management, private or public, will directly influence its use and success.

Caravan Sites Act (1968)

Despite the fact that the Caravan Sites Act (1968) is often referred to as the first piece of significant legislation regulating the provision of accommodation, the trail of evidence about the poor living conditions of

Travellers and Gypsies goes back to before this time. Some of those with whom we consulted during the course of this research suggested that it was the changes to planning laws that were the initial cause of the problems facing Travellers and Gypsies in establishing adequate accommodation and that this remains a key underlying problem today. The Caravan Sites (Control of Development) Act (1960) was highlighted in this respect because it made it virtually impossible for individual families with their own resources to create new caravan sites. According to one of those with whom we consulted:

> If it were not for the 1960 attempt to cut off the development of sites altogether, Gypsy money would have solved the Gypsy problem. That is still the problem. The 1968 Act sought to resolve the problem by further discrimination, providing segregated sites for Gypsies.[13]

Although the Act did also provide local authorities with a discretionary power to set up sites for caravans in their areas, with some limited central government funds available to support their work, uptake was limited with the result that there were actually fewer places – particularly in terms of common and farmland – on which Travellers could station their caravans, except for very short periods of time.

The Caravan Sites Act (1968) attempted to address the issue of accommodation provision by making it a duty on County Councils (to identify sites) and District Councils (to develop and manage them) in the rural shires, and London and Metropolitan Borough Councils to carry out both duties elsewhere to provide a network of public sites for those residing in or resorting to their areas. In return, local authorities that provided sufficient sites were given additional powers of eviction against unauthorised encampments in their area (known as 'designation').[14]

There is considerable evidence that the 1968 Act had a positive impact on the provision of sites. Although this was slower and more limited, especially in the early days after its passing, than had been hoped, a recent report concludes that the Act achieved a significant increase in the number of publicly provided pitches, and that the unauthorised encampment figure had been reduced from 80 to 30 per cent (Morris and Clements 2002). Many of those who responded to the consultation exercise also commented that the Act was not a failure in the sense that the Government has recently suggested. Large numbers of sites were provided, and a larger proportion of young Travellers became literate.

Nonetheless, by 1994 when the Act was repealed, 62 per cent of local authorities had not achieved 'designation', even though a few of those who did not apply for it had enough sites to satisfy their legal obligations under the duty. The duty was not consistently enforced even after 1979 when a 100 per cent grant was offered to cover capital site-building costs. Although the Home Office Minister had the power to direct a local authority to provide such number of sites as was felt fit as a result of the Act, the reality is that this power was not exercised at all in the 1970s and early 1980s. When it was used, albeit sparingly, towards the end of the Act's life, it proved effective. What was lacking was the political will to ensure that the accommodation needs of Travellers and Gypsies were addressed. In addition, although local authorities had been required to provide sites, these were sometimes located in unacceptable areas, for example near rubbish dumps or industrial sites, under motorways and on other marginal land. There is evidence that this had implications for the health of Travelling communities, and that isolation from schools and other facilities reinforced the geographical and social exclusion of Travellers and Gypsies.[15]

Criminal Justice and Public Order Act (CJPOA) (1994)

The new legislation that was introduced in 1994 was the result of a number of different pressures. First, there was a growth in public concern over so-called 'New Age Travellers' camping on unauthorised sites. Second, the Government became concerned about the cost to local taxpayers of providing sites, although this was modest in comparison with the cost of providing 'bricks and mortar' social housing for an equivalent number of families. Thirdly, and perhaps most importantly, the Government was ideologically committed to the proposition that private enterprise – and specifically the purchasing of land by Travellers and Gypsies on which to build their own sites – could satisfy the demand for accommodation.

As a result of these pressures, Section 80 of the Criminal Justice and Public Order Act (which came into force in November 1994) repealed sections 6-12 of the 1968 Act and the grant scheme with which they were associated. The change in policy underlying the repeal was explained by the then Parliamentary Under-Secretary of State in the following terms:

> In the past 13 years the number of [G]ypsy caravans stationed on unauthorised sites has remained broadly the same...The shortfall in provision has been largely due to natural growth in the [G]ypsy population...We believe that public provision has now reached an acceptable level. Public accommodation has been provided for 46 per cent of the total number of [G]ypsy caravans in England and Wales. We do not believe that it is in the public interest to continue to maintain what has become an open-ended commitment to provide sites for all [G]ypsies seeking accommodation at the public's expense. It is our view that the right approach now is to encourage more [G]ypsies to establish their own sites through the planning system. We know that many [G]ypsy families would prefer to establish their own sites rather than reside on council sites... Private site provision has increased by more than 135 per cent since 1981. Our intention is to encourage that trend.

The result of the Criminal Justice and Public Order Act (1994) therefore was to remove the obligation upon local authorities to provide sites for Travellers and Gypsies, and the central government grant available to fund this provision, although local authorities do have the power to do so (under section 24 of the Caravan Sites (Control of Development) Act 1960). Instead Travellers and Gypsies are expected to provide their own sites through purchasing suitable land and gaining planning permission. In order to facilitate this process – and arguably partly in order to reduce opposition to the CJPOA – the Department of the Environment issued a new planning circular (Circular 1/94) which stated that where Travellers and Gypsies purchased their own land, there would be a 'level playing field' in terms of planning permission, and local planning authorities were advised to include a policy on sites for Travelling communities in local plans. Circular 1/94 theoretically puts Travellers and Gypsies on the same footing in planning law as everyone else. It was designed to ensure that applications for Gypsy caravan sites are treated in the same way as any other form of development. It places emphasis on local authorities identifying suitable locations for Traveller and Gypsy sites in their development plans wherever possible. Failing this they should identify clear and realistic criteria for suitable locations as a basis for their site provision policies. Wherever possible, local authorities should encourage Travellers and Gypsies to consult with them on planning matters before buying land on which they intend to camp and for which planning permission would be required.[16]

The problem with this approach to accommodation provision is twofold. On the one hand there is clear and growing evidence that the provisions of Circular 1/94 have not been adhered to and that planning applications from Travellers and Gypsies wishing to establish new sites on land that they have purchased are not dealt with in the same way as other planning applications. Few authorities provide support to Travellers and Gypsies to ensure that they purchase land which is likely to be granted planning permission to establish a new sites and ODPM's own research indicates that hardly any local authorities are identifying specific land for site development. When Travellers and Gypsies do acquire plots of their own, they frequently do not apply for planning permission because they do not understand the issues involved or do not think it will be granted (Niner 2002). The experience of Travellers and Gypsies who do apply for planning permission is almost invariably that they are refused, forcing some families into long and protracted legal battles with no more likelihood of success than before Circular 1/94 was issued. Some families are deeply traumatised by these disputes as some authorities have used unfair tactics to defeat applications. The result may be that those who have the money will not buy because they see their relatives buying what seems to be suitable land, spending considerable amounts of money on planners and lawyers and ending up with no permission. The overall impact is certainly, in a growing number of areas, an increase in private sites that are being built without planning consent. A further problem, however, is that just as all social housing tenants have not been in a position to buy their properties, so too many Travellers and Gypsies do not have the financial resources to purchase land for a site (in the region of £20,000 upwards) and will therefore be reliant upon a pitch provided by a local authority or housing association.

Perhaps most significantly for the purpose of this report, the 1994 Act not only undermined provision but exacerbated existing inequalities and tensions between Travellers and the settled population. At the same time as failing to address the issue of accommodation provision for those who could not afford their own sites (by providing more publicly owned sites), failing to ensure that planning applications by Travellers and Gypsies were treated equally and failing to identify appropriate land on which sites could be developed, the CJPOA also introduced powers for the police and local authorities to move on Travellers and Gypsies even where no alternative authorised sites are available.[17]

To this extent the 1994 Act shifted the centre of discussions about Travellers and Gypsies away from the need to make provision for their accommodation to the question of controlling unauthorised encampments. Although there is a need to ensure that both crime and anti-social behaviour, wherever they occur, are robustly and appropriately dealt with, it is noticeable that this remains the major piece of legislation governing relations between the State and Travelling communities. This is reflected in the fact that both public discussions and policy debates are conducted in terms of criminalisation, public order and anti-social behaviour, rather than in terms of provision, equalities and enforcement of rights.

Current policy and practice

Since coming into power in 1997, the Labour Government has continued to operate within the existing framework provided by the 1994 Act. However, as was indicated at the beginning of this Chapter, the result has been that there are simply not enough places on authorised caravan sites (public and private) to accommodate demand. The overall loss of publicly provided sites and pitches since the abolition of the 1968 Act is, according to some of the responses to the consultation paper, a key feature of the issue since that time. According to government figures there has been a net loss of 596 pitches from authorised sites over the last seven years, representing an average loss of 76 pitches a year (Niner 2002). There has been no significant change in these figures despite the recent central government grant initiative to refurbish sites and provide new transit sites. 157 of all the District Councils and London and Metropolitan Boroughs have had recent unauthorised encampments (which may or may not be unauthorised developments) but no recorded authorised sites of any kind, public or private.

At the same time there is no evidence of a level playing field for dealing with planning applications for sites on land that has been purchased by Travelling communities. Research by the Advisory Council for the Education of Romany and other Travellers (ACERT) found that one-third of councils had no policy at that time (1996/7) on Gypsy site provision in their development plans, and only two had followed the Circular requirement to identify locations for sites (Wilson 1997). The most common approach was to specify criteria that would have to be met before permission would be granted. Follow up research in 1999 found that 90 per cent of planning applications from Travellers are refused compared to 20 per cent of all other applications; on appeal, 63 per cent were dismissed and 28 per cent allowed (Williams 1999). In short, in spite of government guidance in the form of Circular 1/94, Travellers and Gypsies find it very difficult to provide sites for their families.

These difficulties mean that new sites – whether rented or owner occupied – are slow to develop whilst existing sites are being closed completely or are pending refurbishment. Many sites in urban areas are located on land that was marginal and undeveloped, but is now located in valuable regeneration areas. Temporary – but often long-standing – sites are now near high-priced property where opposition to planning permission can be anticipated. The pressure on rural land is increasing with the twin pressures of the Green Belt and the demand for brownfield sites for house building. At the same time some local authorities have commented during the course of the research for this report that the CJPOA was not successful in reducing environmental damage.

This context of on-going historical failure to provide sufficient accommodation for Travellers and Gypsies and to resolve the problems for Travelling communities, local authorities and the settled population has given rise to a significant increase in research, analysis and policy evaluation over recent years. Much of this has resulted from the policy, political and campaigning work associated with the Traveller Law Reform Bill which is perhaps the most important among efforts to legislate for improvement in the provision available to Travellers and Gypsies.

A Private Members' Bill based on work by the University of Cardiff, the Traveller Law Reform Bill represents a broad consensus developed through four years of consultation with a wide range of stakeholders, including Travellers' and Gypsies' organisations, statutory and voluntary bodies such as the police and local authorities, and lawyers and planners who face the problems that arise from the current situation. The major organisations representing Traveller and Gypsy communities have forged the Traveller Law Reform Coalition to campaign for the basic rights of somewhere to pitch a camp and access to basic services and have rallied behind the Traveller Law Reform Bill. This is a unique alliance of Romany Gypsies, Irish Travellers and New Age Travellers who have previously found it challenging to work together, and in the past blamed each other for the loss of sites and the loss of public tolerance.[18]

The centrepiece of the Bill is the reintroduction of a statutory duty on local authorities to 'provide or facilitate provision' of sites where Travellers and Gypsies can live in line with the traditional way of life. The Bill has received support from some local authorities currently wrestling with how to provide sufficient sites and deal with unauthorised encampments, and who feel that the current system of provision means that some local authorities, often in areas where Travellers and Gypsies have traditionally lived or where there are economic incentives to settle temporarily, are disproportionately affected. The second key proposal is a Travellers Accommodation Commission, with 50 per cent representation of Travellers. This agency would oversee the implementation of the duty, as well as 'promote the equalisation of opportunities' for Travellers and Gypsies.

A revised version of the Bill was adopted and read in the House of Commons by David Atkinson MP on 10 July 2002, and was intended to receive its second reading in Parliament on 19 July.[19] However, this was interrupted by a Labour Whip and the Bill fell. Although it was again introduced as a Private Member's Bill in May 2003 it fell again at the end of the last Parliament. It is worth bearing in mind that although Private Members' Bills serve as a useful mechanism for 'airing' issues and securing both a wide consensus and government backing, such Bills have historically enjoyed limited success because they, by definition, are not government bills and generally not able to secure sufficient parliamentary time to progress through all the necessary legislative stages. Importantly however, the Bill has been specifically designed to enable a piecemeal implementation if necessary and appropriate.

Meanwhile, in July 2002, the Office for the Deputy Prime Minister (ODPM) announced its intention to produce a new overarching 'Traveller and Gypsy Strategy' and measures to tackle unauthorised encampments through stronger police enforcement powers linked to improved site provision. The focus of this initiative has been on tackling public concern about nuisance and disorder arising from unauthorised encampments. This announcement was followed by the publication in December 2002 of new *Framework Guidance on Managing Unauthorised Camping* by ODPM and the Home Office. As noted in the guidance, the counts show that most Traveller and Gypsy caravans are on authorised sites and are lawful, and not all unauthorised encampments cause problems for the settled community. However there are a significant number of very problematic unauthorised sites that have an unacceptable impact on the local area. As well as undermining relationships with the settled community, the behaviour on these sites can lead to Travellers and Gypsies being stereotyped and consequently being discriminated against.

The *Framework Guidance* was circulated for consultation and formed the basis of a series of seminars and discussions between many of the parties involved in this issue. It has run parallel to, and has informed, the work undertaken for this report.[20] One of the themes to emerge from these discussions was that the enforcement approach to addressing unauthorised encampment and associated environmental damage was unlikely to be successful because it fails to address the underlying problem of accommodation provision for Travellers and Gypsies. Interestingly, it appears that this concern is shared by a wide range of different stakeholders including some local authorities, groups representing the interests of Travellers and Gypsies, and enforcement agencies including some police.

Nonetheless, the only significant piece of legislation specifically addressing Traveller and Gypsy issues to emerge over recent months has been that contained in the recent Anti-Social Behaviour Act, part 8 of which, when it comes into force in late February 2004, will make it easier to remove Travellers from sites on grounds of trespass, where there are suitable site plots vacant and available locally.[21] There are particular concerns among those from the Travelling community who fear that the use of Anti-Social Behaviour Orders (ASBOs) against Travellers and Gypsies will exacerbate existing prejudices and hostility towards them and that the lifestyles of the majority of Travellers and Gypsies who are simply trying to survive in very difficult conditions will be further affected by enforcement legislation devised on the basis of the actions of the minority. This concern is illustrated by recent comments made by the Gypsy Council:

> Most families on the roadside do behave in a reasonable manner, but it is difficult without secure tenure, without toilets, without dustbins, without electricity, without hot water and baths, without social inclusion, to live like a house-dweller. The councils and the newspapers notice where there is a mess and fail to comment when there is no mess...Even if a group of families behave impeccably under all the above disadvantages, they will *still* be evicted (emphasis in original).[22]

Nonetheless, it appears that the ODPM is taking seriously the evidence emerging from its own commissioned research, from the University of Cardiff, from the Traveller Law Reform Coalition and from a whole range of other organisations and individuals working on or with Travellers and Gypsies. The Government has recently established a policy review within the ODPM to assess the impact of present policy and carry out research. Although some of those who have worked or campaigned in this area for many years are understandably suspicious of what they perceive may simply be an excuse to delay any form of action, it is clear that this issue has moved very firmly onto the Government's agenda.

The commitment by the ODPM to review its Gypsy and Travellers' Strategy may provide a significant opportunity for real change, not least of all because part of the impetus for this review is ODPM's work to review its policies in light of the race equality duty. This review is currently taking place and can therefore be informed by, and benefit from, the increasing national consensus amongst the relevant stakeholders (Traveller and Gypsy organisations, NGOs, think tanks, local authorities and the CRE among others) that resolving the accommodation issue is the most significant problem to be addressed, and doing so successfully should help overcome a number of other barriers to progress in areas such as community relations, education and health. It is also particularly timely given that ODPM are developing and implementing current wider proposals for reform of the planning and housing system. The proposals, launched in February 2003 as *Sustainable Communities: Building for the Future* are designed to ensure adequate provision of accommodation through reform of the planning system; with increased funding for affordable housing; and improved maintenance of existing stock, so that all social housing reaches a decent standard by 2010.

The proposed changes in planning and housing provisions are so far-reaching that they create a real opportunity to locate Traveller and Gypsy accommodation issues as a housing issue, and thereby provide a means for addressing this need into the future. Enabling mechanisms alone will not be effective because of the current levels of local hostility towards the Travelling community. The challenge is to win official acceptance of Traveller and Gypsy accommodation (permanent and transit sites) as a form of housing. Flowing from this, provision could potentially be made through Regional Housing and Spatial Strategies; funding provided via Regional Housing Boards; networks of sites established across local authorities with Regional Development Agency co-ordination. Local authority social housing funding could be made dependent on willingness to provide all housing required including Traveller and Gypsy sites. This report sets out the process by which this might be achieved and the benefits which would result if policy and practice in this area were able to move forward from the approach taken over the last forty years.

Accommodation as key

It seems likely that the shortfall in adequate pitches to meet the needs and nomadic patterns of Traveller and Gypsy communities (including transit sites) has contributed to an increase in unauthorised encampments and has led to increasing concerns about planning approval, trespassing, proper sanitation and waste disposal facilities, environmental nuisance and clearance costs for local authorities agencies. Local authorities continue to have dual responsibilities for controlling unauthorised sites and making adequate provision for sites, but without the correlative link that characterised the Caravan Site Act (1968) duty or any additional resource from central government (with the exception of the recent refurbishment grants) or any national co-ordination or strategy for provision.

There is evidence that this approach, when combined with the fact that patterns of site provision are highly varied across local authority areas, has led to resentment that local authorities who do not make adequate provision, especially if they take a hard line on eviction from unauthorised encampments, are very likely to increase the difficulties for neighbouring authorities that have provided sites. The variation in demand for sites is partly determined by traditional patterns and travel and work. But it may also be influenced by the willingness or otherwise of local authorities to provide sites. In the absence of a coherent national approach to site provision, there is a reluctance among local authorities to provide 'more than their fair share' for fear that this will attract Travellers and Gypsies from other areas of the country who are unable to secure adequate accommodation elsewhere. This fear acts as a barrier to sensible and co-ordinated measures to tackle to problems of inadequate accommodation. Until there is adequate site provision, local authorities and the police will have to continue dealing with the problems associated with unauthorised encampments, rather than proactively meeting need. This is costly and is based on prosecution and enforced movement rather than provision. It may address the presenting problem but it does little or nothing to prevent it. As such, it is a very poor use of resources.

The situation therefore cannot be resolved without the provision of appropriate permanent sites for the majority of Travellers and Gypsies who want to be able to remain for long periods in one area (not least so that their children can attend school) but also requires provision for transit or short-stay sites, so that they can travel when necessary for work or social events. Where residential and transit sites provide toilet facilities and provision for the removal of other domestic waste, one significant cause of tension will be alleviated. The authorities will, moreover, be in a stronger position to address any unauthorised encampments, because there will be alternative legal sites to which Travellers and Gypsies can move; and to deal with the separate issue of fly-tipping and environmental damage.

For local communities to accept authorised sites, they will need to see that provision in their area is proportional to need and matched by provision in other areas; and that the sites are managed in a way that avoids – or remedies quickly – any negative impact on neighbouring areas. Local authorities are under considerable political pressure from the settled community to act firmly and swiftly on unauthorised encampments, particularly where these are associated with environmental damage or where the use of public recreation land is seen to deny access to other users. The settled community will need to see that local authorities have sufficient powers, resources and commitment to deal with the environmental crime associated with unauthorised encampments when it occurs.

As the evidence in the following Chapter suggests, the scale of the problems associated with the current inadequacies of accommodation provision are substantial in terms of the impact on the lives of individuals and families from the Travelling community, in terms of conflict and tensions with – and sometimes impact on the lives of – local settled communities, and in terms of the political and financial costs associated with unauthorised encampments.

5. Why we need to move forward

Despite the lack of coherent and comparable data relating to Travellers and Gypsies, it is clear that as a group they are perhaps more marginalised and more frequently the subject of discrimination and racism than any other ethnic group in the UK. It is also clear that the issues arising, in significant part, from inadequate accommodation contribute substantially to poor health status and educational attainment, to conflict between the Travelling and settled communities, to environmental damage arising from domestic waste and to intense financial and political pressures on local authorities arising from all of the above. As the evidence presented in this report suggests, there are a considerable number of stakeholders involved in this issue and there is a great deal to be gained by all of them from pursuing new approaches, even if initially these may be in parallel to existing approaches. New approaches have the potential to create a win-win situation: the Travelling community will have sufficient accommodation to meet its needs and the health and educational status of individuals and families will most likely improve; for the settled community there will be no more unauthorised encampments with their accompanying (actual and perceived) nuisance and environmental damage; local authorities, the police and the courts will no longer have to carry the burden and expense of dealing with unauthorised encampments and their aftermath. And all of this, combined with fair and even enforcement against unacceptable behaviour (which should be much reduced) from any quarter, will contribute to improved race and community relations between the Travelling and settled communities.

Health

The lack of permanent sites on which to live has clear and dramatic implications for the lives and lifestyles of Travellers and Gypsies. Recent research indicates that Travellers have a high maternal death rate, and quite possibly the highest maternal death rate among all ethnic groups. Traveller women live on average 12 years less than women in the general population and Traveller men 10 years less than men in the general population (Barry *et al* 1987). A number of other research reports looking at a range of indicators of Traveller and Gypsy health provide evidence of inequality and discrimination:

- A range of locally or regionally based and sometimes descriptive studies have indicated higher morbidity levels for Travellers than for the rest of the population (Anderson 1997, Linthwaite 1983, Pahl and Vaile 1996, Van Cleemput 2000).

- Several local or regional studies focusing on child and maternal health have demonstrated high infant mortality and perinatal death rates, and high child accident death rates (Beach 1999, Feder 1989, Hajioff and McKee 2000, Linthwaite 1983, Morris and Clements 2002, Pahl and Vaile 1986).

- Health problems for mothers are shown starkly in the report of The Confidential Enquiries into Maternal Deaths in the United Kingdom which found that Travellers have 'possibly the highest maternal death rate among all ethnic groups' (Lewis and Drife 2001). Less well documented are the health needs of Traveller and Gypsy men.[23]

- There is some evidence that changes to travelling patterns and related impact on lifestyle may have a detrimental effect on quality of life and mental health (Van Cleemput and Parry 2001).

- There is some evidence that Roma refugees and asylum seekers experience a range of health problems associated with pre- and post- migration stresses (Burnett and Peel 2001, Hajioff and McKee 2000, Plafker 2002, Pomykala and Holt 2002).

- Results of a large scale study of Traveller and Gypsy health in England, being funded by the Inequalities Programme in the Department of Health, are not available at the time of this report but will include socio-demographic correlations of health, including different types of accommodation.

Much of this is likely to reflect the inability of Travellers and Gypsies without adequate accommodation to access health services. Travellers frequently have difficulties in registering with a GP due to rejection by GP practices. This is due in part to their mobility (enforced or otherwise), to bureaucracy and paperwork that Travellers often find difficult to understand, and to a lack of cultural awareness and perceived racism on the part of service providers. Evictions from unauthorised campsites make it hard to sustain regular employment, school attendance and regular health checks and means that Travellers and Gypsies – many of whom are forced to go to Accident and Emergency departments to receive treatment – miss out on advice, support and preventative healthcare. There is inevitably a lack of continuity of care as Travellers and Gypsies move (or are moved) from one area of the country to another. Although there are some examples of good practice involving outreach by health visitors there are significant variations in service provision and few mechanisms for sharing good practice more widely.

Anecdotal evidence gathered during the course of this research is reinforced by findings from research studies, from practice accounts and from national working groups on Travellers' health which have identified a range of problems in Travellers' access to health care including difficulties in registering with a GP (and subsequent lack of access to both primary and secondary care), and substandard maternal care. Research conducted by Save the Children (1996) into healthcare for women in Scotland showed that almost a third of the Traveller and Gypsy women interviewed had been refused registration at a GP surgery on one or more occasion. Moreover, there is a substantial body of evidence that the social and political context of Travellers' lifestyles exacerbate health problems including stress and anxiety associated with enforced mobility, lack of basic services and sanitation, low socio-economic status and lack of access to education.

Education

Research studies have consistently demonstrated that Traveller and Gypsy children are seriously disadvantaged in the educational system. A recent Ofsted report (2003) estimates that there are between 10-12,000 Traveller children of secondary school age who are not registered at school. It also states that the average attendance rate for Traveller pupils is around 75 per cent, well below the national average and the worst attendance profile of any ethnic minority group. The findings of forthcoming research from the Nuffield Foundation (to be published in March 2004) will help to explain many of the reasons for secondary age children failing to sustain their attendance.

There are also concerns about attainment levels once Traveller and Gypsy children are in the educational system; Ofsted reports (1996, 1999) have identified Travellers and Gypsies as the group most at risk of failure in the education system and have shown that pupils from Travelling communities are likely to fare badly within schools across a range of measures. Anecdotal evidence suggests that in a context of significant reliance on overall school performance via league tables, some schools are unwilling to register Traveller and Gypsy pupils who are perceived as low attainers. Educational inequality is not only determined by difficulties of access to schools, but also by unequal access to an appropriate curriculum, teacher expectations and cultural support. The most recent Ofsted report (2003) on this issue cites a lack of flexibility in the curriculum, deep-seated prejudice in the community and poor understanding of Traveller culture and lifestyle as possible reasons for the increase in this trend. Bullying has also been identified as a major issue affecting all of the above. For example, the Scottish Traveller Education Project identifies bullying to be an endemic problem in schools in Scotland, and concludes that the failure of schools to tackle this problem causes many Traveller and Gypsy children to drop out of the education system.

Studies have also shown the increased disadvantage experienced by Travellers without an authorised site or other legal occupation suitable for their needs. Families who live on unauthorised encampments can be evicted within days, which make access to education difficult or impossible. There is evidence that, not surprisingly, children in those families who have experienced a series of evictions are the least likely to attend school. Given this picture, any disruption to the schooling of children that would result from eviction needs to be avoided if local education authorities are to fulfil their duties to make school education available and if the children's parents are to be able to send their children to school. In addition, all local authorities have duties under the Children Act (1989) to support children's best interests. Some authorities establish a dialogue with families and avoid unnecessary evictions; in such circumstances children can attend school and enjoy continuity of education although there are wide variations in practice. At the same time however, it is the responsibility of parents to ensure that their children attend school on a full-time basis but with a limited defence to parents whose occupational mobility prevents their children attending the whole year. Given that across the population, secondary age children who are excluded or permanently truant from school are far more likely to be involved in crime and be at risk, there is a clear win-win for community relations if parents, local authorities, schools and the police are able to work together to ensure full-time attendance as an objective. A framework of adequate site provision, coupled with other supportive measures, would provide a secure basis on which to take forward this approach.

Environmental impacts

The issues of accommodation provision and of environmental damage associated with unauthorised encampments cannot be dealt with in isolation from one another. Earlier work undertaken as part of this research and sponsored by the London Borough of Newham's Overview and Scrutiny Unit focused specifically on the environmental impacts of unauthorised encampments and fly-tipping (London Borough of Newham March 2003). Research undertaken by the University of Cardiff has found that for many local authorities, the increasing costs of managing unauthorised encampments are directly linked to site clearance and cleaning up afterwards. In terms of managing the environmental impact of unauthorised encampments, local authorities are faced with challenging and sometimes conflicting duties, and limited resources. The Traveller Law Research Unit surveyed all local authorities about their costs of managing unauthorised encampments in 1998/1999. The 70 per cent of authorities that responded reported expenditure of £6 million. The 30 per cent that did not respond are likely to have had expenditure not dissimilar. In addition the evidence suggests that those who responded underestimated their costs by not accounting for staff time. This survey did not count the costs incurred by government and national agencies such as Forestry Commission, the Highways agencies, private landowners or the police. The authors conclude that it is probably safe to assume that the actual figure of £6 million derived from this research could be multiplied a number of times before the real annual cost of managing unauthorised encampments is reached (Morris and Clements 2002). Not surprisingly, local authorities are concerned that the significant costs of clearing up domestic waste associated with illegal encampments and fly-tipping displace much needed resources from street cleaning, refuse collection and areas of environmental improvement.

Traveller and Gypsy encampments are frequently assumed to be associated with illegal economic activities such as fly-tipping and with waste dumping, particularly in the popular press and amongst local settled residents. One respondent to the consultation exercise suggested that fly-tipping often tends to be blamed on the nearest site, authorised or otherwise, sometimes with perverse consequences:

> When police chase stereotypes instead of actually investigating the crime, the result is not only heartbreak for the victims and failure for the police. The stereotyping actually encourages fly-tipping, because the fly-tippers know that they have only to tip near a Gypsy encampment to ensure that the Gypsies take the blame and that there is no proper investigation of their crime.[24]

Although not all fly-tipping is associated with illegal encampment – indeed the lack of data and monitoring makes it difficult to empirically establish a link between the two – some local authorities (including the London Borough of Newham) do have evidence of such a link. The link between unauthorised encampments and environmental damage (including that associated with fly-tipping) has also been made by the ODPM. This actual and perceived link between Traveller and Gypsy communities and illegal waste dumping activities both gives rise to and exacerbates prejudice and discrimination, and undermines the ability of local authorities to challenge the prejudice that exists towards Travellers. A clear example of this is the recent report by the National Farmers Union (NFU) which crudely estimated losses of £100m to farmers as a result of activities from unauthorised encampments and declares 'illegal' Travellers to be 'rural outlaws'.[25]

A key conclusion of the seminar discussions held as part of the research for this report was the need for a more nuanced understanding of the environmental impact of unauthorised encampments. The environmental impacts of domestic waste associated with unauthorised encampments and fly-tipping (as a commercial activity or as a by-product of trades such as building, laying tarmac, garden waste, scrap dealing and car stripping) stem from different underlying causal factors and therefore require different policy levers. The issue of domestic waste is closely related to site provision. Fly-tipping by contrast is a criminal activity that inflicts huge costs on local authorities and has a significant impact on local residents' perceptions of their local environment and fear of crime.[26]

It follows logically on from this that policy proposals to deal with environmental crime associated with unauthorised encampments must address both the provision and enforcement aspects of this issue in parallel. The proposals in Chapter 6 of this report which establish a mechanism for securing the provision of sufficient accommodation for Travellers and Gypsies will, if implemented, render it much easier to identify, implement and enforce specific policy levers to address environmental impacts associated with waste from unauthorised encampments and fly-tipping. Indeed some of the problems of domestic waste disposal in particular will disappear once adequate site provision has been made. Nonetheless, it is recognised that in order for this to happen local authorities must feel confident that they can deal adequately with the fly-tipping of unauthorised waste where it occurs and that they have the appropriate powers and resources to enable them to do this. This will be vital to maintain the support of the settled community to the provision of permanent and transit camps.

The appropriate policy proposals to deal with domestic waste are therefore intricately related to authorised or unauthorised site provision and management and are dealt with in this paper accordingly. If more authorised sites are provided or facilitated this problem should disappear, because it can be dealt with in the same manner as refuse clearance and sewage is dealt with for the settled community, through the payment of council tax and water rates. Where adequate provision is made and residents fail to maintain their accommodation to a reasonable standard, local authorities should respond in exactly the same way as they would to other tenants in social housing or, if the land is privately owned, in the same way as they would with any other homeowner. This principle is well accepted within the Traveller and Gypsy community.

Several examples of good practice in dealing with environmental impacts associated with waste disposal on unauthorised encampments were identified during the course of this research. The National Romani Rights Association, Norfolk County Council and Kings Lynn & West

Norfolk Council have developed the groundbreaking Frankham Bond initiative to tackle this issue in relation to temporary permitted encampments. A private landowner and recognised Gypsy groups enter into a simple legally binding licence agreement which permits occupation of land for a specific number of days, with a nominal fee paid to the landowner via the local authority. A copy of the licence and the agreed deposit is lodged with the local authority, which provides basic sanitary facilities, running water and waste disposal facilities. In return the Gypsy families agree to keep the site clean, tidy and unpolluted. When the Gypsies leave the site in compliance with the agreed terms, the deposit is returned. If not, it is used to pay for cleaning the site. This scheme was piloted in the summer of 2003. There are also examples of 'toleration agreements' between police, private landowners and Travellers, which limit the number of residents on an unauthorised site, which is then tolerated on the understanding that the site must be kept clean, tidy and unpolluted. A feature of 'toleration agreements' (a term which many Travellers take exception to) is often a commitment to clearing up rubbish on the site before Travellers move on to it, and maintaining it in a clean and tidy state for when they leave; in turn some agreement enables the group to keep out 'strangers' who may fly-tip and cause trouble. This enables the Travellers to have stability in their lives for periods of time so that children can attend school and parents have sustained contact with community development workers. The pressures on the local authority to 'deal with' the situation are simultaneously reduced.

In addition, however, the discussion on this issue at seminars which were held as part of this research led us to the conclusion that a more proactive approach is needed to ensure that unauthorised encampments are monitored and managed in order to negate damaging environmental impacts and reduce the subsequent costs of clear-up. The existing approach to addressing the environmental impact of unauthorised encampment represents a very poor use of limited resources. Good research and data would enable patterns of movement to be identified and transit sites to be located on routes that cross local authority boundaries. A code of conduct, developed through proper and meaningful consultation with Travellers and Gypsies, could be an appropriate policy tool to steer the development of better relations between the Travelling communities and local authorities and to ensure that good practice initiatives can be established where appropriate and practicable. This reflects a concern that responding to an otherwise non-disruptive unauthorised site with eviction does not solve the rubbish problem; it moves it on somewhere else.

One of the considerations that any statutory crime prevention partnerships will have to address is how to investigate, prosecute and take enforcement action against individuals who are transient and who move across council and police boundaries, with no permanent home address. A Traveller living on an unauthorised site can just move on when it appears that the enforcement agency may catch up with them. The benefit of more official sites, offering permanent and regularised accommodation, is that those individuals responsible for fly-tipping can be dealt with through the criminal and civil courts in the same ways as other perpetrators, without the inequitable and discriminatory practice of evicting the whole group of families for the (alleged, but not pursued) criminal activities of one or few individuals. While all Travellers are blamed for tipping, the majority of Traveller households are as dismayed by tipping activities as the majority of the settled community. The implication is that the management of unauthorised and authorised sites must consciously build on the established family networks, which ensure standards of behaviour, and pay attention to the compatibility of Traveller groups sharing a site. These networks are essential to the control of waste and rubbish.

Given the disproportionate impact of fly-tipping – financial and political as well as on relations between the Traveller and settled communities – it is clear that improved policy tools are urgently needed to address this issue. Our research and analysis suggests the need for a two-pronged approach. Firstly, as above, improved site provision to reduce the level of unauthorised encampments and illegal activities. In addition, the regularisation of accommodation will help with crime prevention measures, criminal investigations and prosecutions. And secondly, tougher penalties imposed on those who continue to fly-tip and appropriate policy levers to enforce these are required. The measures are not – and should not be interpreted as being – specific to Travellers and Gypsies but apply universally to all sectors of the community. These two policy approaches will need to be implemented in parallel if they are to be politically acceptable to local authorities and workable in practice.

6. A fresh approach to the provision of accommodation

As has been set out in earlier sections of this report, and echoed in ODPM's own research, there is currently no national policy for ensuring that the accommodation needs of Travellers and Gypsies are met. A lack of overall aims and objectives means that there is a lack of overall direction and fragmentation between agencies often with different portfolios and agendas, and huge variability of 'implementation' geographically (and over time). The current situation is that it is for local authorities to determine whether, how and where sites are provided and permitted (unless an appeal is successful), and that they should enter into voluntary partnerships at district, county or cross-county levels to secure adequate provision. Planning provisions under Circular 1/94 were intended to create a level playing field for planning applications to establish private sites which would prevent any unmet need from arising.

Our research suggests, however, that it is unlikely that local rather than regional site provision strategies will adequately meet the patterns of movements and accommodation needs of Traveller and Gypsy communities. Nor will the enhanced powers to evict Travellers proposed by ODPM prove a sufficient incentive in and of themselves for local authorities to provide new sites and improve existing practice in relation to planning application. Rather, our research suggests that there is a need for new mechanisms to ensure regional partnership working across local authority areas; and that a purely voluntary approach to securing agreement among authorities on the most appropriate location for sites will be unsuccessful. Such mechanisms will need to involve 'carrots' as well as 'sticks', derived from a national and regional assessment of accommodation need (based on better information and data for planning), and include strategic links with education and welfare services, equalities and social inclusion. This approach will also require a decision about who (which body) should have responsibility for policy formulation, implementation and review and how best to involve Travellers and Gypsies fully in the process.

This chapter sets out possible approaches to increase well-managed site provision and reduced nuisance from unauthorised encampments.

These approaches are not hierarchical or mutually exclusive. Indeed, a strategy which includes elements of all of the approaches is likely to be the only one which will both resolve the current situation and provide a long term and more workable policy solution than that which existed prior to the abolition of the Caravan Sites Act (1968) in 1994. There is a real opportunity at the current time to build on the experience since that legislation was introduced, rather than simply replicating it and potentially repeating the weaknesses and failures. There is also the potential for any new system seeking consensus to enhance community relations, reduce tensions and break down ignorance and fear from all quarters.

Obligation to provide or facilitate the provision of sites (temporary and permanent)

Reinstating some sort of compulsion or statutory duty to provide or facilitate the provision of sites is viewed by many as fundamental in helping to tackle resistance from settled communities to local authorities meeting the needs of Traveller and Gypsy communities. Many believe that a statutory duty and central subsidy are needed to 'encourage' local authorities to make provision. The duty would require a local authority either to provide authorised sites itself or to facilitate provision by allocating sites in local plans and looking favourably on applications from Travellers and Gypsies for planning permission for these; and working with private landowners, RSLs or local charities to make such provision.

Arguments for the reinstatement of an obligation to provide publicly owned sites reflect a concern that the ideological commitment to private enterprise and reducing the costs to the public purse of providing sites which underlay the thinking behind the measures associated with the Criminal Justice and Public Order Act (1994) represented a misplaced confidence that Travellers and Gypsies would be able to purchase suitable land to build their own sites. Even without the problems associated with obtaining planning permission, there remains a fundamental belief that publicly financed housing should be available to those that cannot afford to purchase their own accommodation. Many Travellers and Gypsies will never be able to afford their own sites. The need for publicly owned sites is particularly evident in metropolitan areas where land costs are high. Without such sites, real estate costs will push Travellers out of urban areas.

The level of provision needed in each area varies. As part of a national strategy to ensure adequate publicly provided provision, regional requirements would need to be identified by central government in consultation with regional and local authorities. The number of pitches proposed would take into account predicted population growth and new households, current residents who are without a legal place to park, as well as housed Travellers who want to move back to sites. Sufficient transit sites would be included to take account of travelling patterns, and temporary stopping places suitable for seasonal work and traditional events. The grant from central government would reflect the extent of the required provision by each local authority. Travellers and Gypsies would pay a reasonable rent for the time spent at these sites and the local authority would have powers to ensure the proper running of the sites, whether by private, RSL or public management.

Measures that might be taken to 'facilitate' the provision of sites could include tolerating traditional stopping places, obtaining grants for self-build sites, ensuring sufficient planning applications are approved by changing the current much ignored Circular 1/94 with guidance that local authorities must identify suitable locations as well as supporting the construction of sites by Housing Associations. Some of these options can be provided at minimal cost to local authorities. According to research undertaken for ODPM, nearly half of all local authorities have adopted a policy of toleration. However, how this term is understood and what the policy means in practice can vary. Toleration may simply be the time taken to make welfare enquiries and initiate court proceedings, mutual agreement on the date when Travellers and Gypsies would leave the camp or where a blind-eye was turned to situations, such as where a family had stayed in a location over a number of years but without planning permission. Alternatively, a local authority may have criteria, such as location, size of groups, and welfare needs, which provides for toleration of camps for up to 28 days or longer in certain circumstances.

Given the current government drive to increase freedoms and flexibility at a local level, a centrally enforced statutory scheme may not be consistent with government policy priorities, and may not be supported. It would overtly increase central government control over local authorities at a time when it wants to demonstrate that it is decentralising power. Critics of the statutory duty emphasise, moreover, its failure to deliver when on the statute book from 1968 to1994. Responding to the Select Committee's call for the statutory duty on local authorities to be reintroduced the ODPM has stated that:

> The Government is actively considering how best to ensure that local authorities ensure that the accommodation needs of Gypsies and Travellers are met. Whilst the previous duty did result in the creation of some sites, it was not universally successful. Therefore the Government is actively considering the most effective mechanism for site provision.[27]

But there is some evidence to refute the claim that the 1968 Act was failing by the early 1990s when its repeal was proposed by the then Government. As was suggested in Chapter 4 of this report, many local authorities failed to provide sites because of resistance from resident communities, the perceived inadequacy of the grant from central government, and the weakness of the enforcement mechanism or lack of political will to use it. But it needs to be remembered that over 300 local authority sites across England were provided, under the duty within the Caravan Sites Act (1968).[28]

Local authorities are in a difficult position. They face fierce local opposition to provision of sites, yet know that this is fuelled by public reaction to the unauthorised encampments which are the inevitable result of failing to provide authorised sites. Local authorities do not welcome intervention by central government, yet cannot address this problem alone as only a regional solution in which their neighbouring authorities also make suitable provision will reduce the risk of unauthorised encampments. This suggests that it will not be sufficient simply to re-establish a statutory duty of the kind that previously existed, not least because it did not provide either a mechanism for delivery or for enforcement. Rather an alternative mechanism is needed that requires collective action on a regional basis to ensure that sufficient sites are provided. There are a number of good reasons why it might be logical to establish a statutory duty in parallel with this alternative mechanism:

- It would send out a strong message to local authorities from central government and provide local authorities with a substantive answer to local residents who oppose provision.

- Politicians at a local level would be able to use it to justify site construction to their constituents.

- The threat of legal prosecution would provide local authorities with a substantive answer to local residents who oppose provision for failure to comply with a statutory duty and could add a further incentive to local authorities to provide or facilitate.

- The reintroduction of an obligation to provide or facilitate has strong support from Travellers and Gypsies themselves.

There was significant support among those whom we consulted, including some local authorities.[29] However such an obligation will not be successful in meeting need without the mechanisms for ensuring delivery that are proposed in this section and indeed might fall away if the other policy approaches are taken forward and prove successful.

Bring Travellers' sites within the new housing and planning system

One attractive option would be for the Government to bring the provision of sites within its current proposals for reform of the planning and housing system. The proposals, launched in February 2003 in *Sustainable Communities: Building for the Future*, are designed to ensure adequate provision of accommodation through reform of the planning system; with increased funding for affordable housing (around £22 billion between 2002/03 and 2005/6); and improved maintenance of the existing stock, so that all social housing reaches a decent standard by 2010 (ODPM 2003). Under the new arrangements, Regional Spatial Strategies will include allocation of new housing provision for each local planning authority (unitary and district councils) reflecting regional housing need. New Regional Housing Boards will allocate funding to local authorities and to RSLs from a single pot covering both housing maintenance and provision of new social or subsidised housing.

Traveller accommodation should, where possible, be given the same legal status as housing and assessed and delivered in the same manner.

Such a policy would go a long way to combating many of the accommodation inequalities facing Travellers and Gypsies and would also give the Travelling community many of the rights enjoyed by settled householders. At present, however, it is implicit that such provision refers only to 'bricks and mortar' housing, although the homelessness legislation recognises that the lack of a legal place to park and live in a mobile home constitutes homelessness. Apart from the obvious missed opportunity that this could represent, there was also some suggestion from those with whom we consulted that the fact that Traveller and Gypsy needs are currently by default excluded from Regional Spatial Strategies and the remit of Regional Housing Boards is a breach of the Race Relations (Amendment) Act (2000) and could constitute institutional racism.[30]

If Traveller and Gypsy sites were treated as housing, an estimate of need and plans for provision would have to be made as part of Regional Housing Strategies reflected within the Regional Spatial Strategies and implemented by local authorities through their local plans.[31] The site could then be provided either by the local authority itself or by the Housing Corporation through an RSL, a private sector provider or voluntary sector body.[32] A national or regional RSL could indeed be established for this purpose, an idea which is discussed later in this chapter.

If this option were taken forward, it would be imperative, given the history of lack of site provision, that specific funding was ring-fenced for site provision and that there was no possibility for the 'central pot' to be spent on other forms of housing provision. This would need to be explicit. It would also need to be made clear that the quality and suitability of site provision will need to both improve and be made more appropriate to the needs of Travellers and Gypsies if it is to be successful in reducing unauthorised encampment. Current site provision may separate families who have more children than can be accommodated in one caravan so sites that are built should also take into account that plots have room/permission for two caravans on them, to cater for the larger families of Travellers and Gypsies and improve the flexibility of provision to meet local needs. Disabled facilities should be part of the criteria for inclusion into the design and building of future sites. Sites should not be built in or near unacceptable areas such as landfill sites, canals, motorways, train lines or industrial areas. They should include safe play areas for children.

Getting the design and sustainability of sites right will require input from Travellers and Gypsies prior to design and building.

Under this approach, where a local authority failed to make provision for the number of sites of a suitable quality required by the Regional Spatial Strategy, the Secretary of State could issue a direction requiring it to do so, if necessary enforceable in the courts. The danger is that without some sort of sanction the incentive to provide permanent and transit sites would not be sufficiently strong because some local authorities would welcome an opportunity to absolve themselves of responsibility for providing accommodation. One suggestion made during the consultation exercise was that authorities that do not facilitate accommodation provision for Travellers should be penalised in the form of restricted powers to evict and refuse planning permission. This could work as an additional incentive to a financial penalty. The feasibility and practicality of any enforcement mechanisms would need to be explored further to ensure that any sanctions would ensure appropriate accommodation was provided.

Moreover, in this arrangement there would be an alternative, powerful, sanction. If funding for sites were to come within the responsibility of the Regional Housing Boards, resources would be allocated to a local authority, or to RSL or private sector providers, once provision had been made for sites in the local plan. The Regional Housing Board, controlling the local authorities access to funds for all of its social housing, could simply make receipt of some of a local authority's funding conditional on its fulfilling its responsibility to provide necessary sites for Travellers.

Provision of new sites and refurbishment of existing sites to satisfactory standards of accommodation will clearly need new resources. However, as indicated in the previous chapter, research by the Traveller Law Research Unit of Cardiff Law School suggests that costs borne by the public as a result of inadequate site provision may exceed the cost of making the necessary provision (Morris and Clements 2002). Local authorities, the police and the Environment Agency pick up a significant bill not only for evictions but also for the clean up of sites that have inadequate waste facilities. In any case there is no reason why additional resources being made available to provide 'Decent Homes for All' should not extend to Travellers and Gypsies.

Much of what is required to bring Traveller and Gypsy accommodation needs within the existing and forthcoming housing and planning systems does not appear to need primary legislation. Where there is a need for legislation this could be met quickly through the current Planning and Compulsory Purchase Bill and Housing Bill. The draft Housing Bill was published for public consultation and pre-legislative scrutiny in March 2003 and introduced into Parliament on 8 December 2003. Its stated aim is to help the most vulnerable and to create a fairer and better housing market. It contains no reference to the accommodation needs of Travellers and Gypsies. This could be resolved through relatively straightforward amendments to the draft legislation. For example, in order for the Housing Corporation to have resources available to support the development and maintenance of Traveller and Gypsy sites and funding for other types of housing provision for Traveller and Gypsy families and communities, it will be necessary to amend the existing housing legislation to empower the Housing Corporation to make grants to registered social landlords (RSLs) to enable them to provide and manage such sites. Similarly, any enforcement mechanism to create an obligation on local authorities to provide for or facilitate Traveller sites would require an amendment setting out the process by which this would be enforced. Further consideration should be given as to how the objectives of Circular 1/94 can be met and what mechanisms might be introduced in the proposed planning legislation to ensure that Traveller and Gypsy planning applications are treated equitably.

This approach would sit more comfortably with decentralised service provision. It would make clear that Traveller and Gypsy housing needs are central to housing and planning policy, not a separate issue. It would enable a joined-up regional approach that would provide a more consistent level of provision. The funding incentive would be a powerful one. At the same time as mainstreaming Traveller and Gypsy sites into the new housing and planning system it would seem eminently sensible to ensure that other aspects of inequality arising from the fact that the Travelling community is currently marginalised in existing policy across the board is addressed. Adequate accommodation provision would make this possible but arguably local authorities which provide sites should be provided with resources that not only cover the direct costs of provision but that reimburse them for other costs associated with provision, including the costs of mainstreaming the needs of Travellers and Gypsies into other areas for which they have responsibility. Those local authorities that make no provision should be expected to fund a proportion of the cost of providing sites in their sub-region. In the meantime there are other areas that remain to be addressed. For example, security of tenure is widely viewed as a key to developing sustainable communities and social cohesion. Many Travellers possess licences which means in some cases they can be given as little as seven days notice to leave a site in spite of the fact that they and their families many have been living there for many years. Travellers should be given greater tenants rights and encouraged to form tenants' communities and given a greater say in the design and management of their sites. This would require a root and branch reform of Caravan Sites legislation, which is widely acknowledged to be in need of change and would benefit all who live on managed sites (whoever they are).

Create an institutional driver

If any or all of the options outlined above are adopted, it is our view that there will need to be central direction and guidance to facilitate the successful operation of any new systems. A new body should be established with both a consultative and advisory role to collect data on need, advise the Regional Planning Bodies, monitor local plans, promote good practice, pilot new models of provision and so forth. Guidance and pressure from such a body could increase both the likelihood of adequate provision and the standard of sites. Its roles could include:

- Working with police, local authorities and other services, including large landowners such as the Forestry Commission and Crown Agents to identify suitable land for sites;

- Advising Travellers and Gypsies how to gain planning permission for new sites (including prior to the purchase of land for which planning permission may then be difficult to obtain) and how to get support from the new enhanced Planning Aid service;

- Ensuring greater consistency in standards of provision and in the management and regulation of unauthorised sites through information sharing and data provision;

- Collating information about existing good practice in site provision management, and in relation to other strategies for provision of services, for example Homelessness Strategies;
- Collating data on site vacancies and making this information available to regional bodies and local authorities;
- Collecting and analysing statistics on planning applications, refusals and the result of appeals in order to identify those areas in which current planning guidance is not being adhered to; and
- If the Government were to reject the suggestion that provision of sites should be included within Regional Spatial Strategies and funded by the new Regional Housing Boards, this new body could be given responsibility for funding provision and even for the maintenance of sites.

The Traveller Law Reform Bill itself proposes the creation of a new body – the Gypsy and Traveller Accommodation Commission – whose principle task would be to ensure that there was adequate accommodation for Travellers and Gypsies in England and Wales. The Commission would be representative of the organisations concerned, as well as of interested public bodies and voluntary organisations. An alternative to a Non-Departmental Public Body (NDPB) of this kind would be a Travellers Accommodation Service under the auspices of the Government regional offices or the RDAs.

Establishing a new body would, however, take time and resources. Bearing in mind the current central funding for sites, the significance of planning and housing systems that are centrally guided, and the need to ensure site provision within short timescales, our proposed option is a high-level unit within the ODPM, led by a Grade 3 Senior Civil Servant.

Similar to the Rough Sleepers Unit, the unit could be established as part of the Homelessness Directorate in ODPM, which already has expertise in this area, developed through tackling rough sleeping. The unit would be charged with delivery of the necessary number of sites within Local Development Frameworks by 2006/7, and with the related responsibilities for promoting good practice and advice that we have proposed. This unit would be also responsible for ensuring that accommodation requirements are properly understood and measured and that Travellers and Gypsies are properly consulted. Led by a very senior official, the unit would be charged with delivering a target number of well run sites within (say) a three year period. Working through the Regional Planning Bodies (and possibly controlling release of the relevant component of the Regional Housing Board budget for the provision of sites), the unit's aim would be to ensure that suitable sites were identified in all the Local Development Frameworks (local plans), which have to be in place by 2006/7. It might also identify the RSLs capable of providing and managing the sites, or be a catalyst for the creating of a specialised RSL for that purpose. Part of their responsibility would be to ensure that the policy measures that were introduced to ensure adequate provision of sites and accommodation ran in parallel with policy measures to ensure that local authorities had the appropriate powers and resources to deal with environmental crime associated with unauthorised encampments, including through working directly with other government departments.

A unit with this type of leadership and mandate would – in contrast to current arrangements within the ODPM – have both the authority and the incentive to deliver. An evaluation of the Irish Government's National Strategy on Traveller Accommodation has concluded that the lack of central direction was a significant cause of the failure by local authorities to deliver (Irish Traveller Movement 2002). Such a unit could be established at short notice. The motivation, from the Government's perspective, for raising the level of priority attached to this issue by establishing such a unit, would be the real prospect that it could have a significant impact on social cohesion by 2006/7 by removing or reducing the community tension caused by unauthorised sites and the environmental damage to which they give rise.

It would be critically important to the success of such a unit however that, as one respondent put it, 'it doesn't simply become another layer between ourselves and the Minister, with no benefit to us'. In order to avoid this and to ensure that the unit consults effectively with, and learns from, existing experience and expertise within the Traveller and Gypsy community, a Traveller Task Force should be established, comprising a significant proportion of Traveller and Gypsy representatives and other key stakeholders, who would be consulted at an early stage and ongoing, in a meaningful way, on any developments and advise the proposed unit. The dialogue that has been created to date between the Government and the Traveller Law Reform Coalition has been vital for the emerging consensus on how policy in this area needs to move forward. Future policy development needs to build upon that dialogue in order to develop the emerging self-confidence and dynamism of the Traveller and Gypsy community. This will give Travellers and Gypsies more confidence in government and the knowledge that government is listening to the people most affected by their actions and decisions. Because representatives of such a body could be seen as working clearly in the interests of the Travelling community, the information which needs to be gathered about existing and future needs would in all probability be completed more quickly and accurately. Without this, the success of the policy as a whole could be jeopardised.

Develop regional initiatives

As has been indicated throughout this report, our research found that there was a reluctance among local authorities to provide 'more than their fair share' for fear that this will attract Travellers and Gypsies from other areas of the country who are unable to secure adequate accommodation elsewhere. This fear acts as a barrier to sensible and co-ordinated measures to tackle the problems of inadequate accommodation provision.

The logical place to establish any new arrangements might be within some existing organisation like the Regional Development Agencies (RDAs), who already have responsibilities for job creation, skills improvement and attacking social exclusion. As the RDAs are also key organisations promoting inward investment and involved with the business sector (some of whom are major complainants about unauthorised encampments), this could be a useful way of tackling both new site development and the aspects of unauthorised encampment that are damaging to business and business confidence. Providing the RDAs were resourced to do so, they could involve local authorities, housing providers, police, Traveller and Gypsy organisations and others both in overcoming the barriers to establishing sites within the new Regional Spatial Strategies and Regional Housing arrangements. This would ensure that best practice on site development and response to unauthorised encampment will be shared across each Region. They could also seek to identify the locations of highest deprivation and social exclusion and consider the best ways in which health, education, employment and other opportunities, probably at least partly through community development initiatives, could be available to support the independence of those communities and the individuals within them, as well as any associated behaviour aspects. All this activity, subject to the details being sorted out, would arguably fit neatly within current work carried out or promoted by Regional Development Agencies and Government Regional Offices, including regeneration activity.

One way of reconciling this is to encourage site management, as well as assessing the need for provision, on a regional basis. This might well be the approach that a specialised RSL would take (see below). But it has also been pointed out that to do so would be to take a step further away from the related services (education, social services, even the police and 'enforcement' officers who are often the first point of contact for families newly camping in an area), which are largely organised on a county-wide basis. Several respondents to our consultation paper suggested that any new approach should not abandon the County Council role. It was pointed out that many County Councils have an important role to play over and above contributing to any debate on Regional Spatial Strategies not least because in two-tier areas County Councils have provided most existing local authority sites. In areas such as Buckinghamshire, Hampshire and Kent for example, it has been found that the most effective (and indeed cost-effective) way of managing sites is at the county level. However because they are not housing authorities nor yet RSLs, County Councils could not be coerced by demands within Regional Housing Strategies or gain from (or be threatened by the loss of) funds from Regional Housing Boards. It would be remiss to abandon this role for County Councils for the sake of political conformity.

An alternative approach would be to explicitly recognise the county's role, that in this specialised area they have in fact been housing authorities ever since the 1968 Act gave them the duty to provide sites. This would at least clarify the position between district and county. Alternatively they themselves could be recognised as RSLs, either alongside or in place of the specialist body recommended. This would allow existing units to continue and expand in areas where there is a political will for them to do so. This is an issue that needs to be explored further.

Establish a specialised national or regional RSL

We propose this option because the provision of sites is quite a specialist task, involving relatively small numbers of units of accommodation, and it may make sense for there to be specialist Registered Social Landlords who make it their business to provide and perhaps manage these, under the proposed new arrangements. They would also provide an effective alternative to local authorities that were reluctant to make provision themselves.

One model that could be further investigated as a possible model for this approach us that of group housing similar to that which has been developed in the Republic of Ireland and is already being piloted in Northern Ireland. Group housing is defined as residential housing development with additional facilities and amenities specifically designed to accommodate extended families of the Traveller community on a permanent basis. The pattern established is of small groups of purpose-built bungalows or (less frequently) houses in small enclaves, which may or may not include a community house, play areas, stables and grazing and secure work areas, depending on size of scheme, location and Traveller needs. The bungalows (houses) are built to permanent housing standards and are detached or semi-detached so as to allow in-curtilege space for lorries and other vehicles, perhaps including caravans. Properties are rented. Costs of provision are 100 per cent supported by government. According to Niner (2002):

> Group housing, as developed in the Republic of Ireland, proved very popular in principle with Gypsies and other Travellers in our interviews. As in Northern Ireland, it might seem appropriate to run a small number of pilot schemes. In Northern Ireland, pilot schemes are being run by housing associations. The scope for greater involvement of registered social landlords in Gypsy/Traveller accommodation – sites as well as group housing – should be considered by the Housing Corporation.

As was noted above, in the UK the Housing Corporation currently has no power to lend money for the provision of Gypsy sites, and therefore RSLs make no contribution towards the provision of accommodation for Travellers and Gypsies. Group Housing could be an additional option and it should be tried on a pilot scale with government support. The ODPM should seek to promote a partnership between a local authority, a RSL, the Housing Corporation and Travellers and Gypsies in the locality of the local authority concerned, to develop a project as a demonstration model.

Some Traveller and Gypsy organisations are cautious about the idea of a specialist RSL because of concerns that it may not be to the advantage of residents. However the Novas-Ouvertures Group,[33] which has long recognised the need for a dedicated Registered Social Landlord to provide and manage accommodation for Travellers and Gypsies, is highly regarded by many Traveller and Gypsy organisations with whom we have spoken and has recently established Traveller and Gypsies UK (TaG UK). TaG UK will take forward the Group's previous work with Travellers and Gypsies across the UK in the provision and management of supported housing and sites for Travellers and Gypsies. TaG UK currently manages eight Traveller and Gypsy sites in Kent, Sussex and South-East London and is managing two Traveller group housing schemes in Northern Ireland with a total of 13 houses. It may be able to go some way towards supporting the proposals for a dedicated RSL providing and managing sites. The options for this should be explored further.

7. Conclusions and recommendations

This report has set out the issues relating to the provision of accommodation for Travellers and Gypsies including what has gone before, and the consequences of the existing approach for the Travelling community, for local authorities, and for those parts of the settled community affected by unauthorised encampments. It has set out a framework for addressing current and projected need based on the provision of public sites through mainstreamed housing provision and improved planning procedures to facilitate the appropriate development of private sites by Travellers and Gypsies. It has suggested that the solutions to addressing the current inadequacies of accommodation (both quantity and quality) lie in: ensuring that the existing obligations to ensure equality of access to public provision and promote good race relations are properly utilised as a lever for change; in reforms of government planning and housing strategies which can provide a vehicle to ensure that Traveller and Gypsy accommodation needs are properly resourced and enforced; and in the on-going ODPM review of its own Gypsies and Travellers Strategy.

The key conclusions of our research are as follows.

- It is clear that Travellers and Gypsies are currently not sufficiently integrated into existing policies – of both central and local government – which are covered by the Race Relations (Amendment) Act (2000), including Race Equality Schemes, housing and homelessness strategies, planning regulations, social exclusion and community cohesion strategies, community safety strategies and local strategic partnerships. Despite the fact that central government, local authorities and the police are under a positive duty to ensure non-discrimination on racial grounds and to promote good race relations, both Romany Gypsies and Irish Travellers continue to be marginalised from mainstream service provision. Service planning for mainstream activities should take account of Traveller and Gypsy needs at national and local levels. In this context local authorities must include Romany Gypsies and Irish Travellers in the Equalities Standard as a matter of urgency.

- In conjunction with efforts to mainstream the needs of Travellers and Gypsies into existing service provision, local authorities should develop overarching strategies to address the needs of, and issues associated with, Traveller and Gypsy communities which include not only enforcement and regulation but also housing, social care and welfare, education, health and public information and education.

- One of the key concerns throughout this report has been the need to address the tension that exist between Travelling and settled communities. It is this tension that local authorities are required to resolve through their service, planning and enforcement activities. Although the proposals in this paper would go some way to addressing this by tackling the underlying root causes, cases of inappropriate and discriminatory behaviour will doubtless remain. At the present time, ODPM is focussed on ensuring that Travellers and Gypsies conduct themselves properly either through compulsory measures, such as ASBOs, or voluntary agreements, for example, agreed codes of conduct. At the same time however there is also clearly an urgent need to challenge discriminatory behaviours and prejudiced attitudes against Traveller and Gypsy communities by the settled population. This can range from local hostility and negative media coverage, to physical attacks and violence.

- Reflecting this, it is clear that at all levels of the political spectrum there is a lack of political will to tackle the marginalisation of Travellers and Gypsies in society and to address the impact that this has both on these communities and on those local authorities who are expected to provide support without any additional resources or political leadership from central government. The discourse is one of enforcement and eviction rather than provision, and Travellers and Gypsies are viewed by many as a problem rather than a social group in need of support. Underlying this is a failure to accept the nature of the nomadic life style and provide services which suit it.

- It will not be possible to mainstream provision for Travellers and Gypsies and tackle the causes of discrimination and marginalisation until there is better data and information about the needs of Travelling communities, the numbers in local authority areas, and patterns of movement within and between regions. This data should be sufficiently detailed and nuanced to enable an analysis of the differences between rural and urban areas, between different types of authorised and unauthorised encampment, and between different groups of Travellers and Gypsies (including by gender, age and life cycle).

- In order to understand and respond appropriately to the needs of Travellers and Gypsies it is essential that meaningful consultation is undertaken with them when formulating policy solutions. Because of their nomadic lifestyles, Travellers and Gypsies present particular challenges when engaging in consultation, inclusion and engagement strategies.

It is clear from the research undertaken for this report that any lasting and forward looking policy solution will need to be one that:

- Recognises the entitlement of Travellers and Gypsies like other residents to accommodation which, in their case, includes sufficient services, both permanent and transit;
- Provides a funding mechanism where specific funds are channelled into providing suitable accommodation for Travellers and Gypsies, similar to other forms of social housing;
- Establishes a mechanism for enforcement which provides rewards as well as sanctions to local authorities;
- Recognises the challenges for local authorities but overcomes any inertia or resistance;
- Enables joined-up regional accommodation provision;
- Allows flexibility of accommodation types to meet a range of needs;
- Is underpinned by a thorough needs assessment, building in projected needs;
- Facilitates the widespread identification and dissemination of good practice; and
- Is supported from initial outline to implementation by active involvement and meaningful consultation with Travellers and Gypsies.

Conclusions and recommendations

We do not underestimate the scale of the challenge involved in addressing the issue of providing accommodation for Travellers and Gypsies. We have, indeed, been here many times before. However, even during the course of the research undertaken for this report the centre of gravity has shifted quite considerably. There are new opportunities ahead to make real and sustainable progress on the key issue of accommodation provision. Our specific recommendations are:

- Permanent residential and transit sites should be classed as housing, for provision to be made through Regional Housing Strategies and Regional Spatial Strategies, and for funding to be provided through Regional Housing Boards; and for Regional Development Agencies to co-ordinate and lead local authorities in establishing networks of sites across each Region, dependent on evidenced need;

- Local authorities thus should be required to make provision for sites within their Local Development Frameworks; for Regional Housing Boards to make receipt of funding for social housing dependent on an authority's willingness to provide the full package of housing required, including locations for suitable Travellers' sites;

- The sites are be established and run by local authorities, RSLs, private or voluntary bodies;

- A specialised national or regional RSL should be established for that purpose;

- This agenda should be driven forward by a high-level unit within the ODPM, led by a senior civil servant, charged with delivery of the necessary number of sites within Local Development Frameworks by 2006/7, and with the related responsibilities for promoting good practice and advice that we have proposed;

- This unit should be advised by a Traveller Task Force comprising a significant proportion of Traveller and Gypsy representatives and other key stakeholders, who would be consulted at an early stage and ongoing, in a meaningful way, on any developments and advise the proposed unit; and

- Local authorities should include Romany Gypsies and Irish Travellers in the Equalities Standard as a matter of urgency and to ensure that all other local strategies include a recognition of – and response to – the needs of Travelling communities. It would be advisable for both local authorities still needing to produce Homelessness Strategies and those that already have produced these strategies to review them to ensure full compliance with the requirements of the Race Relations (Amendment) Act (2000).

We recognise the challenges faced in ensuring equality of opportunity and treatment for Travellers and Gypsies in the absence of systematic baseline data and limited recording. However in addition to the excellent work on Needs Assessment in Northern Ireland, a number of English councils, including Sevenoaks, Basildon, Hertsmere and adjacent authorities, South Bedfordshire and others are pursuing similar approaches to identify current and future accommodation needs. The Centre for Urban Studies at the University of Birmingham is currently advising the ODPM on the whole issue of the half-yearly counts, with a report, it is understood, to be published imminently, and this is welcomed. We are also aware that whilst accurate monitoring is essential if differential outcomes are to be fully identified and changes made, many Travellers and Gypsies have deep-rooted fears about identifying their ethnicity and are often reluctant to give information to local government officers, even if is of a fairly general nature. As a result of suspicion and hostility families may give different answers to questions about their accommodation needs and aspirations depending on the officer asking the question. Our proposal for an independent Traveller Task Force which includes a substantial proportion of Traveller and Gypsy representatives advising the proposed high-level ODPM unit may be able to help overcome some of these issues involved in data collection and therefore help generate better needs assessment.

On the basis of these proposals we envisage that site and housing needs could be identified within the next two years and serve as a basis for work in identifying site locations and building sites over, say, the following two years until 2006/7. The systems for Regional Spatial Strategies, Regional Housing Boards and necessary funding make the provision of an increased number of the further necessary residential and transit sites during the next four years a realistic target. In the meantime there will continue to be a significant number of Travellers and Gypsies unprovided for, many of whom are living on the roadside and whose children are at a critical stage in their education and development. An interim strategy should be drawn up to address these immediate needs.

Whether or not our conclusions and recommendations prove to be workable and are taken forward depends, in our view, on the political commitment to resolve the inadequacies of Traveller and Gypsy accommodation provision once and for all, and the willingness to grasp the nettle. To this extent the willingness to use and enforce the mechanisms which any policy development in this area could establish are as important as the mechanisms themselves. The ideal would be that sanctions are not needed, because self-interest and cost savings drive the efforts successfully towards better quality and more accommodation to meet simple needs.

Part of any unwillingness to take forward our proposals may arise from concerns about the risks of a new approach to this issue. But the risks of not addressing the issue are arguably much higher, in terms of the costs of managing unauthorised encampments, possible risks of public disorder, costs of crime and of addressing environmental damage. Principal among the risks is the human cost to Travellers and Gypsies themselves, and to the communities in which they live, including on their life expectancy, health and education, and relations with the settled community. But there is also the continuing risks for those from other communities of not knowing where encampments or developments may be set up, nor what the impact may be on neighbours. Over the long term all of these risks threaten to undermine wider government strategies for community cohesion.

The proposed legislative changes in planning and housing are so considerable that the opportunity presents itself for tackling this long-term vexed issue more effectively in the future. We would urge the relevant government departments to reflect on these careful, considered, but different approaches in keeping with the 21st century. We envisage that considerable benefits will flow from a fresh approach if implemented with care and firmness, not only in terms of better quality accommodation and quality of life for Travellers and Gypsies themselves, but for the wider community and for local authorities.

Endpiece

Significant, and one has to say, almost novel historically, is the level of consultation that ippr has had with Gypsy and Traveller representatives and organisations, as well as site visits to view the matter at first hand. Particularly satisfactory to us in the Traveller Law Reform Coalition (TLRC) is the high level of recognition accorded to us as the main and broadest based representation of Travellers in Britain today.

2003 was, generally speaking, not a happy year for Gypsies and Travellers. Sadly, that year saw what most believed from the evidence was the racially motivated murder of Johnny Delaney, a teenage Traveller, who was attacked in the vicinity of an unauthorised encampment, where members of his family lived and whom he had been visiting. In court proceedings the judiciary were technically unable to identify a racial motive, and punish the perpetrators accordingly. The case could have set important precedents, but the chance was lost. For Travellers, the case has the same symbolic importance as the Stephen Lawrence case. In 2003, pressure from the continual horror of homelessness and unauthorised encampment evictions continued to mount, seemingly unaddressed by those who should have the responsibility to provide, namely the local authorities.

Despite the desperate shortage of sites (residential and transit) local authorities and the police continued to evict Travellers into the endless repetitive cycle of illegality. New police powers in 2003 contained in the Anti-Social Behaviour Act gave cause for worry that widened the chances of abuse of the system to achieve evictions. 2003 also saw the astonishing burning of Gypsy effigies at the Firle bonfire celebrations. That, too, would have slipped by un-noticed but for the courage of a lone woman, herself of Romany descent, who made a complaint and brought the matter to the attention of the media. Fortunately, in this case, the Traveller Law Reform Coalition were able to take the moral high ground, and, instead of being vindictive, sought, successfully, to draw out the possible positives from the event. Meetings with local authority leaders, and with local MP Norman Baker brought positive results in reconciliation, and the signing by Norman Baker MP of our Early Day Motion in parliament, calling for more Traveller sites.

Happily, there were also things to celebrate in 2003. The political movement is still in a forward direction, with slight, though increasing, recognition of the validity of our case from all quarters. Of major importance, and probably the highlight of the Traveller Law Reform Coalition's year, was the fringe meeting held in Bournemouth at the time of the Labour Party Conference, organised jointly by ippr and the TLRC. The meeting was a great success, and many fresh alliances were formed or existing ones strengthened at that meeting. The CRE, Children's Society, ippr, TLRC, and other agencies formulated a cohesive approach to bring pressure for change to the Housing Bill, to include Gypsies and Travellers within its remit, so that they can be treated in an equally appropriate way as are the rest of the population.

We in the TLRC welcome the involvement of the ippr. We feel encouraged by their genuine interest and close attention to the Gypsy/Traveller voice in an effort to find and formulate a resolution to current difficulties that is fair to all parties, both the Travelling and settled communities. ippr has an influence on policy that reflects the quality of its recommendations. It is our fervent hope that they and the Government can bring forward policies that will end the current discriminatory and unequal state of affairs that is unsatisfactory to all concerned.

Len Smith
Traveller Law Reform Coalition
Len Smith is a Gypsy and lived a nomadic lifestyle with his family until the 1970s, which ended with him moving into a council house against his will because it proved impossible to live a nomadic way of life. Len is the author of 'Romany Nevi Wesh' (An Informal History of the New Forest Gypsies) and cultural adviser for the Romany Museum at Poulton's Theme Park. He is a leading member of the Traveller Law Reform Coalition and a respected elder of the Traveller and Gypsy community.

Endnotes

1. As was pointed out by several of the respondents to the consultation paper, this report represents only one of a multitude of different research reports and guidance that has been published both by central government and by a wide range of other organisations and individuals working on these issues. Many view this as a most poignant indicator of the failure of past and current policy to adequately address the needs of Traveller and Gypsy communities, and fear that current efforts are simply an extension of that which has gone before – well-intentioned but ultimately ineffective in delivering change.

2. For further information see www.cre.gov.uk/media

3. It should be noted that this report is concerned principally with the need for, and provision of, sites in England and Wales.

4. It is recognised that there are variations in the use of terminology to describe Gypsies and Travellers. This report uses the term 'Travellers and Gypsies' throughout although it is recognised that the term Gypsy-Traveller is commonly used in Wales, whilst Gypsy Traveller is often used in Scotland.

5. This report does not cover New (Age) Travellers or Occupational Travellers (fairground, circus and waterway communities). Part of the reason for this is that the CRE's statutory remit enables it to focus on discrimination that affects racial groups, and not wider social groups. However, as with their own recent strategy document, the conclusions of this report in relation to the provision of adequate accommodation for Travellers and Gypsies and efforts to improve media coverage and public attitudes, should impact positively on all those in Travelling communities.

6. Communities Scotland is a Scottish Executive agency. Its aim is to work with others to improve the quality of life for people in Scotland by regenerating disadvantaged communities and helping deliver better housing. See www.communitiesscotland.gov.uk for further information and to access the report.

7. The Audit Commission also assesses performance through the Equality Standard self-assessment framework, reported as a Best Value Performance Indicator.

8. When the Disabled Facilities Grant (DFG) was extended to people living in caravans (by the Regulatory Reform (Housing Assistance) (England and Wales) Order 2002), it was pointed out by Lord

Avebury that it was drafted so as to apply to people who live in 'qualifying park homes', in other words people who live on a protected site within the meaning of the Mobile Homes Act (1983), and thus excluded Travellers and Gypsies. As a result the current Housing Bill contains a provision extending the DFG to people who live on Gypsy sites.

9   See www.homeoffice.gov.uk/docs2/cc_guidance.html

10 Section 175 (2) of the Housing Act (1996) states that a person should also be considered homeless if they have accommodation if 'it consists of a moveable structure, vehicle or vessel designed or adapted for human habitation and there is no place where [s]he is entitled or permitted both to place it and to reside in it'.

11 Johnny Delaney was a teenage Traveller who was attacked in the vicinity of an unauthorised encampment, where members of his family lived and whom he had been visiting. On 28 November 2003 two youths were found guilty of manslaughter following his death. Many Travellers and Gypsies were disappointed that the judge felt the attack was not racially motivated. Commenting on the verdict Trevor Phillips, Chair of the CRE, said that 'there has been some measure of justice in this ruling, though it is extremely hard to see how this particular killing wasn't motivated in some way by racial prejudice.'

12 The Gypsy Council considers this to be an underestimate and believes that around 30 per cent of the Travelling community now live on unauthorised sites.

13 Comments made by Professor Thomas Acton, Professor of Romani Studies at the University of Greenwich and Chair of the Labour Campaign for Travellers' Rights.

14 In Circular 49/68 however, Ministers made it clear that designation should not be used in a way that would allow local authorities 'to drive [G]ypsies out of their area, to become the responsibility of neighbouring authorities, in the period before a countryside network of sites is established.'

15 In 1977 a significant opportunity for accelerating the provision of a national network of sites that was provided by John Cripps' review of the working of the Caravan Sites Act was lost. The Cripps report recommended that central and local government should agree a national plan specifying the number and location of sites. This would have been the only way of ensuring that, after discussion, local authorities would have shouldered the right proportion of responsibility, and would have seen clearly that others were expected

to do the same. This was never implemented. Cripps also recommended a 100 per cent grant from central government which was implemented and undoubtedly did increase the site provision.

16 It should be noted that two other departmental Circulars were also introduced which could have made the issue of accommodation provision for Travellers and Gypsies far less problematic had they been adhered to. Circular 18/94 from the Department of Education advised local authorities to be humane and sparing in using their powers of eviction, and drew attention to local authorities' obligations under the Children Act (1989). The circular also suggested that councils could tolerate unlawful sites if they were not causing harm or nuisance, and pointed out how nuisance could be reduced through the provision of skips or toilets. Home Office Circular 45/94 advised police officers to take account of the welfare of older people, disabled people, and children when directing people to leave a site under Section 61 (S61) of the 1994 Act (see below).

17 Section 61 (S61)gives the police powers to require Travellers to vacate land, where there is evidence that they intend to stay there, and there has been damage to land or property, threatening behaviour or there are more than six vehicles. Section 77 (S77) enables local authorities to require Travellers to leave any land in its area if it is occupied without the owner's consent; this applies even if there are less than six vehicles.

18 The Coalition includes The Gypsy Council, The Irish Traveller Movement, Friends, Families and Travellers and the Labour Party Campaign for Travellers' Rights.

19 It is worth noting that Atkinson is a Conservative MP and Vice-Chair of the All Party Group. To the surprise of many he adopted this approach following a large scale unauthorised encampment on a playing field in his Bournemouth constituency over Christmas 2001, which led to a demonstration of protest by the settled community. Atkinson is concerned about the welfare of Travellers but also feels very strongly about the inconvenience caused by unauthorised encampments for the settled community. He believes that the provision of accommodation is the key to both issues.

20 It should be noted that representatives of Traveller and Gypsy communities do not feel that they were adequately consulted about the contents of the Framework document.

21 At present, under the 1994 Act, the police can remove Travellers from private land when there are six or more vehicles on the land.

Under the new amendment, the Government proposes to reduce this so that the police can remove Travellers with two or more vehicles on the site.

22 Extract from a letter from Anne Bagehot to Hazel Blears MP, dated 26 November 2003. There are also concerns that Part 8 of the Anti-Social Behaviour Bill will be ineffective on its own terms; ASBOs can only be effective when a family stays in an area and receives help but Travellers and Gypsies will simply be moved on.

23 The Men's Health Forum (MHF) have recently published a booklet by Richard O'Neill entitled *On the Road to Better Health for Travelling Men*. Copies of the booklet can be downloaded at www.menshealthforum.org.uk

24 Comments made by Professor Thomas Acton, Professor of Romani Studies at the University of Greenwich and Chair of the Labour Campaign for Travellers' Rights.

25 Although the NFU's sample of 2000 farmers was statistically robust, they then simply multiplied the figures estimated by those 2,000 across 270,000 farmers in England and Wales, and, without any independent checking of the material supplied, produced a headline figure of £100 million in annual loss.

26 There are a number of incentives to fly-tipping and most of these are economic. Fly-tipping occurs because the costs of legitimate waste disposal are significant (approaching £100 a tonne in many local authority areas) and soon set to increase. A large proportion of this cost is the result of increased landfill taxes levied by central government in an attempt to minimise waste as part of an overall environmental target. There are relatively large numbers of low-income households in many local authority areas and some of them are willing to fly tip or pay unlicensed operators to dispose of the waste cheaply.

27 See ODPM (2003) The Draft Housing Bill – Government Response Paper, para 69, available at www.odpm.gov.uk.

28 The CRE is also inclined towards the view that the Act in itself could have been highly effective if there had been adequate funding from the start and also adequate enforcement action taken. The benefits of this approach are reinforced by the fact that, after four years of detailed discussion and consultation between Travellers and Gypsies and their representative organisations, the conclusion was that a statutory duty should be reintroduced, and this was put forward in the Traveller Law Reform Bill.

29 This support was particularly evident during the first seminar (before the alternative proposals which are outlined in Chapter 6 were discussed) but was also evident, though to a lesser degree, during the second seminar.

30 The CRE has also expressed its concern that by excluding Travellers and Gypsies from a piece of legislation which aims to provide decent homes for all ethnic groups in the settled community, the ODPM risks failing to promote equality of opportunity or to adequately address potential racial discrimination. Good race relations are unlikely to be promoted if improvements are seen to be offered to certain groups, excluding others.

31 This would follow the arrangements in Northern Ireland, where the Northern Ireland Housing Executive has both strategic and management responsibility for all Traveller and Gypsy accommodation including specifically designed grouped housing, permanent sites and transit sites.

32 This is the technical name for social landlords that are registered with the Housing Corporation (most are housing associations, but there are also trusts and co-operatives) to provide social housing. RSLs run as businesses but do not trade for profit. As local authorities often have a limited supply of housing, they may work closely with RSLs to provide additional housing as well as manage temporary accommodation properties on their behalf.

33 The Novas-Ouvertures Group is an RSL that comprises 14 member organisations whose services include work with rough sleepers and homeless families, Travellers and Gypsies, people from black and minority ethnic backgrounds, asylum seekers, young people and those with offending histories. Novas-Ouvertures is pioneering the move away from the traditional 'welfare' model of service provision into a 'partner facilitator' role of working together with individuals and communities through social enterprise initiatives to enable them to achieve their potential.

References

ACERT & Wilson M (1997) *Directory of Planning Policies for Gypsy Site Provision in England* Bristol: Policy Press

Anderson E (1997) 'Health Concerns and Needs of Travellers' *Health Visitor* 70, 148-50

Avebury E (2003) *Travellers and the Homelessness Act* Available at www.travellerslaw.org

Barry J, Herity B and Solan J (1987) *The Travellers Health Status Study: Vital Statistics of Travelling People* Dublin: Health Research Board

Beach H (1999) *Injury Rates in Gypsy-Traveller Children* University of Wales College of Medicine MSc in Community: Child Health Dissertation, University of Wales College of Medicine

Burnett A and Peel M (2001) 'Health Needs of Asylum Seekers and Refugees' *British Medical Journal* 322

Cemlyn S (1998) *Policy and Provision by Social Services for Traveller Children and Families* Bristol: University of Bristol

Cornwell J (1984) *Improving Health Care for Travellers* London: Kings Fund

DEFRA (2002) *Living Places: Powers, Rights Responsibilities* London: DEFRA

DETR (2001) *Count of Gypsy Caravans* London: DETR

Feder GS (1994) *Traveller Gypsies and Primary Health Care in East London* London: PhD thesis, St Thomas's Hospital Medical School, University of London

Hajioff S and McKee M (2000) 'The Health of the Roma People: A Review of the Published Literature' *Journal of Epidemiology and Community Health* 54

Leigeois JP (1987) *Gypsies and Travellers* Strasbourg: Council of Europe

Lewis G and Drife J (2001) *Why Mothers Die 1997-1999: The Fifth Report of the Confidential Enquiries into Maternal Deaths in the United Kingdom* London: RCOG

Linthwaite P (1983) *The Health of Traveller Mothers and Children in East Anglia* London: Save the Children Fund

Irish Traveller Movement (2002) *Charting a Future Strategy for the Delivery of Traveller Accommodation*

Kenrick D and Clark C (1999) *Moving On: The Gypsies and Travellers of Britain* Hatfield: University of Hertfordshire Press

London Borough of Newham (March 2003) *Unauthorised Encampments and Associated Illegal Activity: Scrutiny Commission Final Report* Available at http://apps.newham.gov.uk/eminutes/new/cabinet/270303/reports/ep203.doc

Mace R (1997) *Monitoring of Traveller Education Projects* Keynote address to ACERT Conference, September 1997

Morris R & Clements L (eds) (1999) *Gaining Ground: Law Reform for Gypsiesand Travellers* Hatfield: University of Hertfordshire Press

Morris R & Clements L (2002) *At What Cost? The Economics of Gypsy and Traveller Encampments* Bristol: The Policy Press

Niner P (2002) *The Provision and Condition of Local Authority Gypsy/Traveller Sites in England* London: ODPM

Ofsted (2003) *Provision and Support for Traveller Pupils* HMI 455 Available at www.ofsted.gov.uk

Ofsted (1999) *Raising the Attainment of Minority of Ethnic Pupils* London: Ofsted Publications Centre

Ofsted (1996) *The Education of Travelling Children: A Survey of Educational Provision for Travelling Children* London: Ofsted Publications Centre

ODPM (2003) *Sustainable Communities: Building for the Future* Available at www.odpm.gov.uk/communities

ODPM (2002) *Framework Guidance on Managing Unauthorised Camping* London: ODPM

ODPM (Nov 2001) *Monitoring the Good Practice Guidance on Managing Unauthorised Camping* Housing Research Summary 150 London: ODPM

Pahl J and Vaile M (1986) *Health and Health Care among Travellers* Canterbury: University of Kent

Plafker K (2002) *The Social Roots of Roma Health Conditions* Available at www.eumap.org/articles/content/90/903

Pomykala A and Holt S (2002) *Romani Women: A Priority for European Public Health Policy* Available at www.eumap.org/articles/content/90/903

Save the Children (2001) *Denied a Future? The Right to Education of Roma/Gypsy and Traveller Children* London: Save the Children Fund

Stonewall (2003) *Profiles of Prejudice: The Nature of Prejudice in England* London: Stonewall/Citizenship 21 Project

Van Cleemput P and Parry G (2001) 'Health Status of Gypsy Travellers' *Journal of Public Health Medicine* 23 (2)

Williams T (1999) *Private Gypsy Site Provision* Harlow: ACERT

Appendix 1:
Round table seminar participants

Susan Alexander	Friends, Families and Travellers
Ann Bagehot	The Gypsy Council
David Bailey	Fenland District Council
Jake Bowers	Romany journalist
Cliff Codona	National Travellers Action Group
Janie Codona	National Travellers Action Group
Martin Collins	Office of Kevin McNamara, MP
Richard Crawford	London Borough of Newham
Jason Dedman	Office of the Deputy Prime Minister (ODPM)
Harbinder Dhaliwal	Local Government Association (LGA)
Peter Goward	University of Sheffield
Bryn Griffiths	London Borough of Newham
Bill Forrester	Gypsy Unit, Kent County Council Social Services
Nolette Keane	Irish Traveller Movement in Britain
Tony Lakey	Norfolk County Council
John Lowe	London Borough of Newham
Rachel Morris	Traveller Law Reform Unit, Cardiff Law School
Pat Niner	University of Birmingham
Emma Nuttall	Friends, Families and Travellers
Gill Prangnell	Cambridgeshire County Council
Matthew Pullen	North Wiltshire Constabulary
Andrew Ryder	Labour Party Campaign for Travellers' Rights
Geoff Robinson Council	Traveller Management Unit, Milton Keynes
Frieda Schicker	London Gypsy and Traveller Unit (LGTU)
Malcolm Smith	London Borough of Newham
Peter Smith	Local Government Association (LGA)
John Usher	Race Equality Unit, Home Office
Siobhan Walsh	Office of the Deputy Prime Minister (ODPM)
Roy Watkinson	Environment Agency
Nicholas Williams	London Metropolitan Police
John Wilson	Novas-Ouvertures Group

Ronny Wilson   Commission for Racial Equality (CRE)
Rod Witham   Norfolk County Council
Margaret Wood   West Mercia Police

Appendix 2:
Responses to the consultation paper

Thomas Acton	University of Greenwich
Susan Alexander	Friends, Families and Travellers
Ann Bagehot	The Gypsy Council
Rodney Bickerstaff	Labour Campaign for Travellers' Rights
Cliff and Janie Codona	National Travellers Action Group
Richard Crawford	London Borough of Newham
Angela Drakakis-Smith	
Terry Holland	Buckinghamshire Country Council
Donald Kenrick	The Gypsy Council
Richard O'Neill	Gypsy Traveller
Pat Niner	University of Birmingham
Frieda Schicker	London Gypsy and Traveller Unit
Seamus Taylor	Commission for Racial Equality (CRE)
John Wilson	Novas-Ouvertures Group
Tom Wiltshire	Leeds City Council
Margaret Wood	West Mercia Constabulary

Appendix 3
Labour Party conference fringe event participants

Mike Aaronson	Save the Children Fund
Eileen Ashbrooke	Neil Stewart Associates
Anne Bagehot	The Gypsy Council
Rodney Bickerstaffe	Labour Campaign for Travellers' Rights
Father Joe Brown	Irish Traveller Movement
Dave Cannon	ACERT/Southwark Traveller Education Project
Cliff Codona	National Travellers Action Group
Janie Codona	National Travellers Action Group
Martin Collins	Office of Kevin McNamara, MP
Jessica Crowe	London Borough of Hackney
Farzana Hakim	Commission for Racial Equality (CRE)
Alison Harvey	The Children's Society
Robert Home	Anglia Law School
Claude Moraes	MEP
Julie Morgan MP	All Party Parliamentary Group Traveller Law Reform
Mike Penn	Labour Party Office, National Assembly for Wales
Trevor Phillips	Commission for Racial Equality (CRE)
Simon Redfern	Connect Public Services
Jane Robson	West Mercia Constabulary
Andrew Ryder	All Party Parliamentary Group Traveller Law Reform
Charles Smith	The Gypsy Council/Labour Campaign for Travellers' Rights
Len Smith	Traveller Law Reform Coalition
Patrick South	Shelter
Paul Stinchcombe	MP
John Wilson	Novas-Ouvertures Group
Margaret Wood	West Mercia Constabulary